Human
SPACES

*Life-Enhancing Designs for
Healing, Working, and Living*

ROCKPORT

Acknowledgments

As all creative work, this book was influenced and shaped by many people. For their unconditional support and encouragement, I am truly thankful and wish to acknowledge:

My contributors, whose blind belief in the project and willingness to participate gave life to the idea;

Wayne Ruga, my *new* old friend, who so willingly shared his wealth of knowledge on the subject and did so with heart;

Rockport Publishers, for their insight and willingness to move the project forward, in particular, Rosalie Grattaroti, whose enthusiastic belief and intuitive understanding never wavered, and Jeanine Caunt, for her patience, laughter, and straight talk.

My family and friends, for their optimistic enthusiasm, especially, Mary Dent Crisp, my mother, and Annie Crisp, my sister, whose almost daily words of inspiration were at times a buoy; Marc Montry and Maureen Zrike, treasured friends, who provided a keen editorial eye in the eleventh hour; and Max Underwood, my partner in life and work, whose brilliance, insight, and valued critique gave sustenance to my work.

First published in the United States of America by
Rockport Publishers, Inc.
33 Commercial Street
Gloucester, Massachusetts 01930-5089
Telephone: (978) 282-9590
Facsimile: (978) 283-2742

Distributed to the book trade and art trade in the United States by
North Light Books, an imprint of
F & W Publications
1507 Dana Avenue
Cincinnati, Ohio 45207
Telephone: (800) 289-0963

Other Distribution by
Rockport Publishers, Inc.
Gloucester, Massachusetts 01930-5089

ISBN 1-56496-432-9

10 9 8 7 6 5 4 3 2 1

Design: Wren Design
Front Cover Image: Lourdes Legorreta
Back Cover Images: *(top)* Moore Ruble Yudell; *(bottom right)* Paul Ferrino; *(bottom left)* Bill Timmerman

Printed in China.

Human
SPACES

Life-Enhancing Designs for Healing, Working, and Living

GLOUCESTER MASSACHUSETTS

ROCKPORT PUBLISHERS

Barbara Crisp

Contents

Introduction

"There is architecture, and it is the embodiment of the unmeasurable."

Louis I. Kahn

Talks with Students

World culture is fast becoming aware of and dedicated to issues that surround its overall health and well-being—mental, physical, and spiritual. This awareness is grounded in a renewed respect for and understanding of our connection to nature and of the connection that exists between mind, body, and spirit. We are seeking sources of healing and renewal to mend the fragmentation of contemporary culture and create meaning in our lives. Our desire to enhance the quality of life is being translated into an ever-widening array of arenas, including the built environment. Our environments must begin to respond to the condition of increased depersonalization within global society due to the stresses brought about by today's living conditions, and the resulting psychological and physiological consequences. Gradually we are developing an understanding of the link between consciousness and our built world, as research continues to indicate that our environments indeed affect and influence our behavior and shape our actions, thoughts, and emotions. As a result, the design professions are emerging with a new awareness about design, building, and living that reconnects mind and body, fostering a sense of place and time and true well-being.

I define the concept of a life-enhancing environment as a place built or created to support and sustain the well-being of a particular occupant of time, place, and culture, where the body as a whole, both inner and outer, is regarded as essential to how the space is experienced. Terms such as *healing environment* and *sustainable environment* are often used to describe a particular environment or use, but rarely are they clearly defined and made specific, accessible, or quantifiable to the observer.

Photo: Moore Rubel Yudell

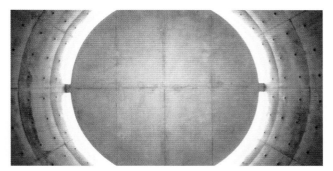

Photo: Tadao Ando Architect and Associates

As an extension of the proposed definition, I offer a set of characteristics or evolving principles that speak to the nature of life-enhancing design. By no means should they be considered dogmatic or part of a paint-by-number formula. They are prescriptive in nature and can be observed in trends emerging in contemporary culture, striving to instruct and to inspire a design sensibility that honors the earth and translates into all aspects of daily life.

Body Centered/Image Object Centered

Our world today is surrounded by and infused with an overabundance of media imagery that diffuses any sense of local culture or place. Detached from natural phenomena, we struggle to find some understanding of the relationship between body and built form. Our bodies articulate our relationship to the world around us. How we perceive space relates directly to body size, its acuity, range of motion, and intention. How one moves through space and interacts with its geometric forms and sensory stimuli defines the realm of our experience of a specific environment or place. This dynamic relationship with the environment is the basis for manifesting an architecture that privileges the person and is body centered rather than place or object specific.

Multisensory/Single Sense

Our senses connect us intimately to the world through the relationships of mental and physical phenomena to our inner and outer perception. What we see, hear, smell, taste, and touch, and what our mind perceives, spans distance, culture, and time. Daily we absorb our surroundings with some intermingling of senses. Each sense has its definitive role to play as part of a collective message, but all too often the senses are considered in isolation. When thoughtfully orchestrated, the sensory experience can provide the underlying essence or spirit of a place. When the sensory experience is consciously intensified, a resulting psychological and physiological dimension can be engaged, elevating the experience of daily life. In many circumstances the tactile, aural, and olfactory experiences can be more a part of one's overall perception of an environment than the presence of visual form. The experience of buildings and environment must go beyond the visual or any bias of a single sense to embrace the visceral depths of multisensory experience. This is not a funhouse of senses, but an articulation of elements that allow the senses to evoke a set of feelings and a level of richness that provides new discoveries and insight on subsequent encounters.

Natural/Synthetic

Our contemporary lifestyles find many of us hermetically sealed within meaningless environments most of the day. We breath artificial air, sit in partitioned space or glass offices, and interact with machines and technology more than with people. Our senses become dulled and canceled by synthetic materials and methods, abandoning virtually any link to the natural world. As human beings, we long for meaning in our lives and in the places that we inhabit. We have an inherent craving to connect with nature, allowing us to temporarily shed the chaotic thoughts and ways of contemporary culture. Architecture and design have an interactive relationship with nature beyond

Photo: Douglas P. Reed, ASLA

topography and site. The primeval forces—sun, wind, earth, and water—and nature's seasonal cycles and rhythms all have a critical relationship to how one experiences space. Elements such as natural light, unrestricted views of and access to the outdoors, and the use of natural materials, are aspects that enrich our environments and allow them to hold deeper meaning.

Sense of Place/Homogeneity

The environments we inhabit should transcend the physical and functional and fuse with the surroundings, creating a place that is specific and unique. Like individuals, every environment should be celebrated as unique. An extension of a particular culture or place, life-enhancing design does not mimic or try to be symbolic, but positions itself beyond style in a deeper realm where the essence of place is revealed through individual experience. Design that proposes gratuitous imitations from a region or era, something that is fashioned and applied as cake decoration is hollow and seeks to impose a generic, singular idea about place. A conscious recognition of and responsiveness to factors such as the surrounding environment, topography, plant material, climate, local materials, cultural history, and people and their beliefs enables the inherently unique design of a place to unfold. To disregard what is appropriate for a specific place, use, and people is to deny that our environments are sacred and have meaning in our lives— mentally, physically, and spiritually.

Duration/Immediacy

Our world is consumed with the instantaneous, the simulated moment, as we channel surf through our daily lives unaware of how the environments we inhabit affect us, offering no conscious resistance. Duration has a critical effect on one's perception of an environment based on the opportunity for discovery and the experiences that are revealed over time. An environment that unfolds slowly to the participant as part of a discovery process, versus seeing it in an instant, touches us, at a deeper level with value and meaning. The use of physical contrasts within an environment, such as up and down, in and out, front and back, near and far, create a dynamic experience that involves mystery and a sense of exploration. The suspense of moving through a space, allowing it to slowly unfold or the celebration of a specific time of day, observing how light falls and shadows are cast, are experiences that enter the realm of the metaphysical and poetic. The spaces we inhabit should evolve through use, through procession, and with the cycle of each day and each season, offering a sense of mystery and wonder, encouraging one to return time and time again.

Photo: Todd Eberle

Photo: Helen Degenhardt

Collaboration/Ego-Centered Design

A collaborative method of working, of insight and implementation, serves to reinforce the foundation for creating a life-enhancing environment. Collaboration erases the traditional disciplinary boundaries and limits, providing new opportunities of empowerment for the client and the participants. Bringing together individuals from the arts, humanities, and sciences, as well as craftspeople, fabricators, and manufacturers expands potential through interdisciplinary expertise and the sharing of ideas. This method of working enables participants to take on new roles, to share values and vision, and to fully engage in seeking appropriate and meaningful design solutions.

The projects selected for inclusion in this book, although diverse in type, share some or all of these characteristics and one required programmatic goal—an acknowledged understanding of and a sensitivity to aspects of healing, human perception and interaction, and well-being, initiated by either the client or the design firm.

In the broadest sense, our environments, the places we inhabit, are part of the stream of events that shape our world and ourselves. Our environments can and should be seen as agents for transformation, providing what is needed to balance the human spirit—support, nourishment, and peace of mind. To arrive at a place and find peace is extremely rewarding, yet rare. These moments are an essential part of life experience and we need more of them.

The Origin and Future of Life-Enhancing Environments

Wayne Ruga, AIA, FIIDA
Founder, President, and CEO
The Center for Health Design
Martinez, California

The interesting thing about money, judging by what most people say about it, is that there is too little of it, they don't have enough of it, they owe too much, or things cost too much. What I think is interesting about money is that it is a precisely calibrated barometer that clearly shows what the priorities are of those who make the decisions about how to spend it. This metric applies across all currencies throughout history.

Interestingly, the same point is true for the essential nature of the manner in which the built environment is developed. Understanding this point is crucial to guiding a project toward its most successful resolution. It is not a question of how much or how little, rather, it is a question of spending what is available on that which matters most.

Another interesting phenomenon is how the highly specialized nature of things in today's world causes us to think of events as singularly isolated happenings. In reality, all events consist of a cause, the actual event, and its effect. To truly understand the significance of an event, we must be able to ascertain its entire continuum.

The same is true for the built environment. To only discuss the physical aspects of a building is to remove it from its context. A building should not be viewed independently from the factors that caused it to be built. When we discuss a building as only a building, we lose the ability to comprehend what it truly is.

Of course, the same can be said for the entire spectrum of built environment elements—from rooms to cities in any culture, at any time. The continuum that enables us to better comprehend the built environment consists of the entire spectrum of conceiving, planning, designing, building, operating, maintaining, and modifying.

Having stated this, the purpose of the built environment is to enable us to best accomplish what the environment was developed for. Beyond the most basic role of providing shelter, we develop environments to facilitate certain predetermined functions. They are places where we can live, work, learn; and places where we can be with our families, interact with others in our communities, participate in sports, obtain health care, and be inspired.

One way of looking at these specific places is to see them as artifacts that reflect the values of the cultures that created them. From this perspective, we gain insight into the priorities and values of that culture. The highest level culture is one that values the dignity of the human being. When this is the case, all aspects of the conceiving, planning, designing, building, operating, maintaining, and modifying environments are done in a manner that supports each human being in expressing his or her greatest potential in the ways that are unique to each and every individual. This is what life-enhancing design is, where it comes from, how it is sustained, and what it causes.

Life-enhancing design is not a style; it has no formula; and it is, by its very nature, not necessarily more costly than any other type of design. It may or may not be pretty, formal, elegant, expensive, or "green." Rather, it is generated by certain intentional values and it causes human lives to be enhanced as a result.

Now, having one's life enhanced is a deeply personal and highly individual experience. Yet, when it happens, we know it. We can feel it in our molecules. Having felt it, our experience is transformed—certainly in the moment, but perhaps even forever after.

Each one of us has the ability to make certain choices. Given our understanding of environment as artifact, as a reflection of culture, representing values and priorities, and causing human lives to be transformed; why would we not choose to encourage a new, more desirable future that causes life-enhancing environments to be the norm? Why would we not choose to seek out life-enhancing environments to be the places where we allow our bodies to spend time? Why would we not choose to cause a future that the result of which would be having our lives—and those of the subsequent generations—be the best that they can possibly be?

This is the opportunity that Barbara Crisp's book makes available to us. It is an opportunity that is too good to not take advantage of—now.

Residential Spaces

Through the centuries, humankind has experienced many forms of the house. From the crude huts of primitive civilization to the modern structures of contemporary times, the house has been more than merely a shelter. It has been a family nucleus, a stage for domestic ritual and celebration, a container for personal possessions, a reflection of self, and a mirror of social conditions and values. Today, as people are trying to cope with multiple demands and ever-expanding information technology, the house has come to symbolize a form of retreat for the restoration and regeneration of mind and body. Of all things, the house should be an environment that sustains and enriches the individual through sensory experience and perception, providing a link to nature, its cycles and materials.

Out of necessity, primitive people were connected to nature in the most fundamental sense. They constructed their shelters of the earth and formed their daily rituals around it. As this traditional shelter was refined over time, ceremonies were introduced to honor the house's organic and mystical connection to nature, providing tradition for succeeding generations. As shelters continued to be perfected and standardized, many cultures moved toward conformity and homogeneity. The connection with nature, its cycles and materials was pushed aside for new technological comforts and status.

...the house has come to symbolize a form of retreat for the restoration and regeneration of mind and body...

Today, this link to nature is not so unfamiliar to our materialistic worldview. We experience the same cyclical signs: the last rays of a setting sun, a full harvest moon, the burst of green buds as winter turns to spring, the long day-lit hours of summer, the clean smell of rain-drenched air. Yet, for many, the experience is unconscious as we dart about, our bodies and minds overcome with the fatigue of day-to-day living. We nevertheless crave this link with our natural surroundings, longing for ways to weave meaning into the places we inhabit. The home should offer such a place—a setting for fostering enrichment and meaning,—for our house is our corner of the world.[1]

However, the home designed to be a part of everyday life yet serving the deeper needs of love, sustenance, and creating a place in the world, is unusual today. If our homes are truly extensions of the self, then we must understand how the body senses, perceives, and inhabits the space in and around the environments we build. There must be a conscious connection to nature and its rhythms. The use of natural materials, rich colors and textures, subtle qualities of light, care and attention to details, the simplicity of form, and a merging with the surrounding landscape are all elements of contrast that inspire the mind, spark the imagination, and delight the body. These are the essential elements that pull us toward broader and deeper possibilities of meaningful dwelling and living.

[1] Glaston Bachelard, *The Poetics of Space*

View from The Wimberley Home of Healing
Wimberley, Texas
Photo: Fabrizio DaRold

Casa Victor y Jacinta

MEXICO CITY, MEXICO

In Mexico, we used to say that the most difficult work of an architect is his own house. Maybe it's because you have to deal with the most difficult client of all... or maybe because it is there, where you are free to explore all your ideas and use all the different materials and forms you have seen in your life.

Victor Legorreta

The site of the house, on the outskirts of Mexico City, is 60 by 100 feet (18 by 30.5 meters), with a very steep slope along one edge. In order to achieve the views and orientation that were critical to the design, the house was developed around a central courtyard, enabling the main rooms to capture sunlight from the south. The wonderful quality of interior light is created by the thoughtful placement of windows to views of the courtyard, the natural environment, and the sky. The use of simple, straightforward materials enables each volume of space to read with equality.

Designed by Victor Legorreta, the son and partner of Ricardo Legorreta, Casa Victor y Jacinta consists of a series of contemporary, minimal

Off the central courtyard a shallow pool provides the soothing sound of flowing water that can be heard throughout the entry level of the house.

All photos: Lourdes Legorreta

spaces that can easily be transformed based on use and need. Daily rituals, such as working, eating, resting, entertaining, reading, playing, and watching television, occur throughout the public realm of the house and are not confined to one formal space. As the immediate needs and ideas of the occupants change and evolve, so does the artwork, furniture layout, and specific functions of the rooms.

The entry to the house is through a high ocher-colored wall that faces the street; it leads to the central courtyard. A fountain and shallow pool provide the soothing sound of flowing water that can be heard throughout this level of the house. A large room off the courtyard is divided by a low wall, creating three distinct public environments, each with its own character and functional relationships. The private areas of the home are separated by a level change and incorporate views to a garden terrace.

The house is designed around a traditional central courtyard. The calming sound of running water echoes off the four surrounding walls, providing a wonderful place for family meals, parties, and a safe play area for children.

The dining room is linked to the living room and hallway through the use of a partial wall. Color, other than off-white, used to partially define the space, is used sparingly on the interior of the house.

*The compressed volume and use of materials creates a sense of mystery
and draws one from the courtyard to the entry of the house. A small
opening in the adjacent wall offers a view of a small side garden.*

The use of hand-painted tiles lends a feeling of antiquity to this modern kitchen with vaulted ceiling and natural light.

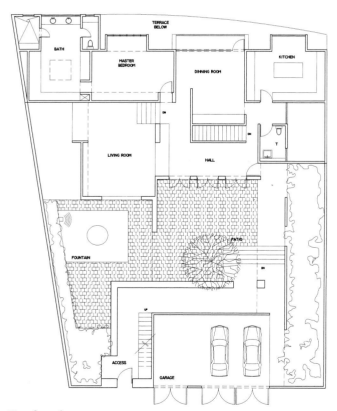

First-floor plan

Credit: Legorreta Arquitectos

Light, shadows, and the use of subtle colors create a beautiful backdrop for the simple, monolithic stone washstand.

The living room has a strong visual connection to the court-yard and adjacent garden space. Filled with books, sculpture, and wonderful light, this space is where the family gathers for television, music, and reading.

The Wimberley Home of Healing

WIMBERLEY, TEXAS

The Wimberley House of Healing sits very deliberately among the cedar trees in the hills outside Wimberley, Texas. The structure has a strong basis in the repetitive use of the golden section, numerology, and feng shui. It opens on the west, protected by wide porches, to the view and sound of gardens and water. The owner, an energy healer, worked very closely with the architect early in the design process in conducting an energy reading of the site. "The topography, the trees, the view, the sun, the stream, ponds, and waterfall, all have something to say and shape the outcome. It's a gathering place of sorts, for subtleties of energy flux." The outcome guided the building program to "envelop the healing energies of the existing site and magnify them to a specific point of focus."

At critical nodes, curved native stone walls are placed through and around the home, creating pools of kinetic energy similar to the Native American webbed dream catchers. Floor levels, corresponding to the energy chakras of the body, step down the gently sloping site and culminate in the transformation room, the energy center of the house. A curving stone wall zones the house into two areas, living and therapy, and acts as a dam for the cascading energies that are funneled into the transformation room through a ribbon window of rose-colored stained glass. The irregular geometry of the stone wall and the 14-foot (4.3-meter) ceiling height create an environment with low levels of echo and reverberation, allowing music to play an integral part in the healing process. In this room the energy healer acts as a channel, directing the flow of universal energy (*chi*) into and through her clients. An adjacent exterior contemplation court contains and reflects any additional chi through the use of a curved stone wall that steps upward.

Great care was taken to ensure that materials used resulted in a safe, nontoxic environment. The home is built of wheat straw bales from Colorado and stucco colored from the local ground stone. Stained concrete, wool carpet, and nonsynthetic paint compose the interior palette and blown biodegradable cellulose insulation insulates the roof. Rain is captured in a system of gutters and ushered into underground cisterns. The Wimberly House strives to be an environment that is healthy to live in—mentally, physically, and spiritually.

Niches are carved out of straw bales on the south wall of the Transformation Room. High clerestory windows are tapered to allow light to fall into the room and subtly wash the treatment table.

All photos: Fabrizio DaRold
All plans and drawings: Living Architecture

The entry foyer displays the power of light. When one enters the home, the eye is drawn upward toward the second floor and on into the sky.

Patios to the west provide transitional shaded space between the house and the pool, creek, and waterfall in addition to screening the harsh western sun.

A vertical stained-glass window captures the chi and funnels it into the Transformation Room and outside to the Contemplation Court where it is contained and refocused by a curved stone wall.

The stone catchment wall at the front of the house traps energy inside. The private spaces shut themselves off from street views and sound with high clerestory windows.

Historical overtones of Victorian mingle whimsically with the Texas vernacular wraparound porch. Existing Live Oak trees influence much of the building's geometry.

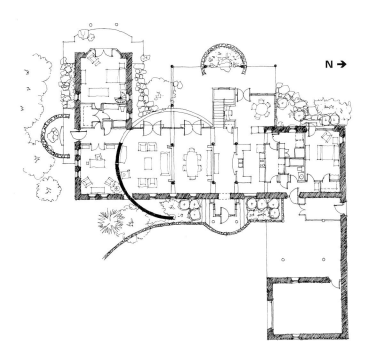

Floor plan

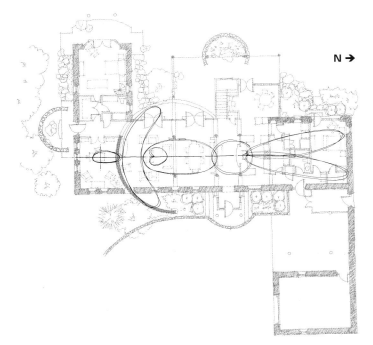

The floor plan with a human-body overlay represents the relationship between the seven energy chakras and the room layout.

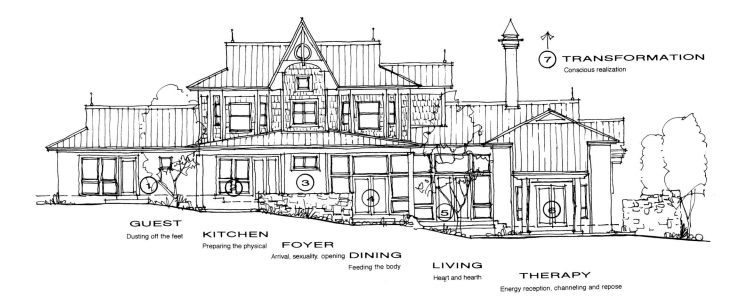

(7) **TRANSFORMATION**
Conscious realization

GUEST
Dusting off the feet

KITCHEN
Preparing the physical

FOYER
Arrival, sexuality, opening

DINING
Feeding the body

LIVING
Heart and hearth

THERAPY
Energy reception, channeling and repose

The elevation of the house reflects the relationship to the seven energy chakras of the body.

The kitchen is located under a sky-lit foyer 45 feet (14 meters) high; it receives direct southern light. Considered a prominent space, the kitchen has sight lines to all other spaces.

Eastern light enters the Transformation Room from a glass-block slit window between the stone catchment and straw-bale walls. The convex geometry of the stone wall does not allow energy to escape and refracts sound waves.

Cox-Lindsey Residence

WAKE FOREST, NORTH CAROLINA

The Cox-Lindsey home is built on what was once the site of a Native American encampment. The colossal trees and natural spring, which are native to the site, remain untouched to honor this mystical place. Leaving natural elements intact is a gesture of respect to the site as a place for retreat and contemplation.

The healing qualities expressed in this multilevel home are rooted in the basic human need to connect with nature. This core connection to the natural environment holds restorative values, enabling one to reduce the level of tension and stress experienced in daily life. The promotion of health and prosperity for both the inhabitants and the Earth is expressed through the use of feng shui, natural and recycled building materials, low volatile organic compound (VOC) finishes, and solar considerations. Each room in the house aligns directly with the cardinal points of the compass, taking full advantage of the sun's movement through the southern sky. The choreography of sunlight begins with the morning sun washing the breakfast deck, spilling into the living room in the afternoon, and completing the cycle as the sun sets outside the bedroom windows in the evening. Large operable windows provide a strong visual link to the surrounding natural environment in addition to cross ventilation. The stack effect, a result of the open air treads and risers between floors, creates a natural vertical air pattern throughout the house. Exposed wood trusses give the main living space a sense of openness, exaggerating the wonderful quality of natural light.

A gratifying compliment came to the owners from a friend who lived with them for several weeks while undergoing breast cancer treatment: "I feel so healthy and alive in your house."

Above:
Dark gray slate, native to North Carolina, provides stepping stones to the entry. The exterior of the house features vertical wood siding with nontoxic sealer, metal roofing, and low-emissivity glazing.

Left:
Skylights allow natural light to flood the open stairway to the top level. An open entryway to the study captures southern light and a view to the treetops.

All photos: Michael W. Cox

The roof overhang and second-floor bedroom deck provide maximum solar gain during the winter months and needed protection in the summer. The large windows optimize year-round vistas, reaffirming the connection to nature.

Site plan:
Direct alignment with the cardinal points—north, east, south, and west—correlates spaces and activities with the sun's movement and provides a connection to the natural cycles of the earth.
Credit: Gail Lindsey, AIA

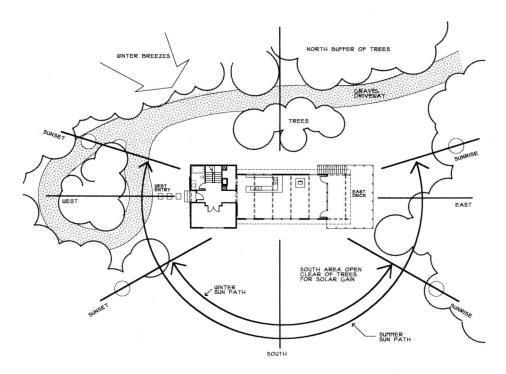

Kitchen cabinets were custom-made, avoiding the use of pressed woods that contain formaldehyde and toxic glues. Water-based sealers were used to finish all wood trim and flooring.

Operable windows, placed effectively on the north and south end of the open living space, provide excellent cross-ventilation in addition to maintaining indoor air quality.

The open metal stairway creates a stack effect. Air flows up and out; fresh air is drawn in, providing natural cooling in the summer months.

The Norwegian wood stove with catalytic converter provides an effective, energy-efficient heat source for the open living room space.

Erle House

GUILFORD, CONNECTICUT

Located on the Connecticut shoreline, this once rambling bungalow acquired numerous additions over its fifty-year history, creating dark rooms that were isolated from the beauty of the natural surroundings. The owner, a violinist of Japanese heritage, chose to remain in the house after the death of her husband but wished to create a new environment that reflected joy and light. It was important that her heritage and her love for the violin be incorporated throughout the house with the use of local building techniques and resources. The intent was to open up the house to views of the surrounding landscape and provide opportunities for sunlight to brighten the interior.

The solution is a contemporary home that blends the character of traditional Japanese construction with the country buildings of southern Connecticut. In an effort to keep the budget small, the original roof was left intact. An entry porch and flower wall were added to define the entrance to the house. Contributing to a sense of lightness and transparency, the relocated entry provides views through the house to a large window wall that overlooks the backyard. The use of wood beams and columns, which extend across the main living space to the outside, further enhance the visual connection to the landscape. Fabric ceiling panels resembling the sensual shape of the violin were hung through the living room to absorb and muffle the sound generated by the predominantly hardwood surfaces. At night the panels reflect the artificial light, creating the effect of a softer, more dappled natural light.

Creating a sense of belonging, a sense of place that embodies memories as well as newness was important in the Erle home. The character of the post-and-beam detailing recalls local barns and stick-style houses of the area as well as traditional Japanese farmhouses. Reminiscent of the Japanese shoji screen, interior doors were designed using wood and rice-paper panels set in standard American pocket door frames. Wood-and-glass wall sconces resemble Japanese lanterns and add subtle light to the living environment. The curves of the kitchen cabinets favor the profile of the violin and all interior wood is held together with bronze pegs symbolic of violin keys.

The bottom half of the bathroom window provides privacy, while the top furnishes views and ventilation. Wood and glass wall sconces were created to resemble Japanese lanterns.

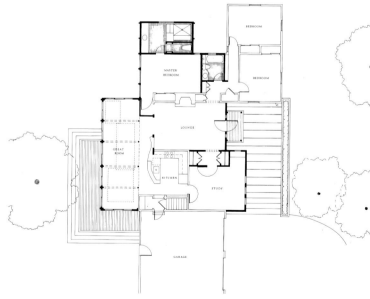

Ground-floor plan

All photos: Jeff Goldberg/ESTO
All plans and drawings: Centerbrook

The house prior to renovation.

Natural wood beams and columns reflect the surrounding wooded site. The large living space provides a bright and open environment that reaches out and becomes part of the landscape.

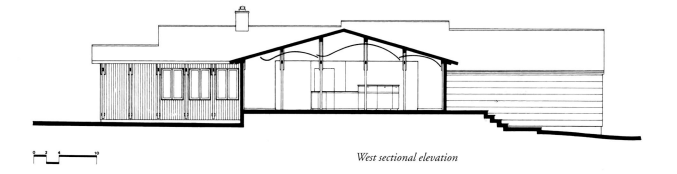

West sectional elevation

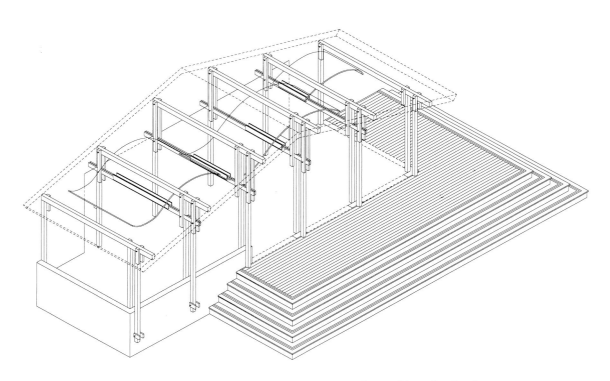

Post-and-beam framing diagram

The kitchen, finished in white ash, overlooks the living room. The interior doors recall traditional Japanese shoji screens, using standard pocket doors with rice paper sandwiched between glass.

Top:
An entry porch and flower wall were added to define the entrance to the house and to create a street-side sitting area.

Below:
The living room opens to the surrounding landscape. Fabric ceiling panels, diffusing light and sound, have curves similar to those of a violin.

House on Mount Desert Island

This house was designed as a prototypical healthy house to meet the stringent requirements of a person with severe multiple chemical sensitivities. The design imperative was to produce a living environment free of harmful substances such as formaldehyde, polycarbonates, and polyurethanes, and with provision for purging the environment of allergens such as dust, mold, and airborne pollutants. In addition, the materials and construction of the house had to be as ecologically responsible as possible. The design needed to express the freedom from discomfort the client's new environment gave her. She wished to celebrate her delight in the space where she could move without pain, without shortness of breath, and enjoy her physical being. The surrounding landscape, natural light, and the daily and seasonal passage of time were important sources of pleasure to her as well.

The client's objectives were addressed through the choice of materials and the configuration of required spaces. An entire rethinking of residential construction was necessary, as the use of many customary building materials were precluded. The solution is a structure of welded steel tubes (both chemically inert and recycled) clad in an aluminum and glass skin (chemically inert and recycled) with floors of maple (a non-endangered species) over lightweight concrete in which all wiring and radiant heating tubing are sealed. The spaces within the house, except for the bathrooms and closets, are configured as open shelves suspended within a steel grid and defined by their spatial separation and geometry rather than by partitions. This allows the air exchange for purging pollutants to occur without costly ductwork and with a minimum of mechanical ventilation. The desire for an expansive feeling within a small house was achieved by the openness of each "room" and the experience of moving from shelf to shelf via the suspended metal stairs or glass elevator.

At different times of the day and at different seasons, the house changes from a transparent prism camouflaged by nature to an opaque object set in the landscape.
Photo: Paul Warchol

Photo on facing page: Paul Ferrino

All plans and drawings: Peter Forbes and Associates

The house rises on the brow of a hill, disturbing little of the natural environment. A grove of white birch trees was planted on the same grid as the house structure to mediate the transition from human-made to natural.
Photos, right and below: Paul Warchol

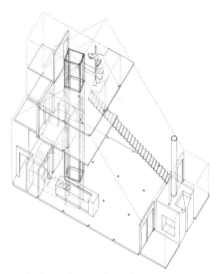

Spatial relationships and circulation

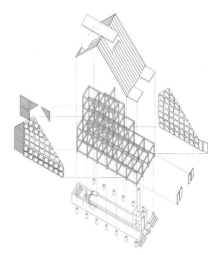

Structure and enclosure

Above:
The third-floor bedroom has the feel of a treehouse, with views to the tops of trees and the partial enclosure of roof and railing.

Facing page:
On the second level, the elevator is enclosed with a finely perforated metal screen that acts as a theater scrim.
Photo: Paul Ferrino

At an oblique angle to the structural grid, the main
stair establishes a grid of circulation that serves to
orient the elevator and the spiral stair above.
Photo: Paul Warchol

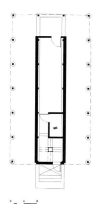

Foundation plan

First-floor plan

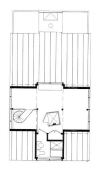

Second-level plan

Dormer plan

Facing page:
The strong geometry of the grid defines different
living areas within the larger envelope. There is a
distinct sense of spatial difference between the
cube of space occupied by the dining table and
that by the fireplace.
Photo: Paul Ferrino

Memory Room

SEATTLE, WASHINGTON

Situated on 2 acres (.8 hectares) of forest land on the edge of a ravine, this 600-square-foot (55.5-square-meter) breakfast room addition was inspired by the memory of a glassed-in porch in the client's childhood home. The room contains familiar objects and treasured items from the client's life, intended to evoke healing reflection and memory for her, a woman suffering from Alzheimer's disease.

The addition takes the form of a box projecting away from the main body of the house and floats over the ravine in the treetops like a tree house. The room captures large quantities of natural light and magnificent views. Throughout the day, a wonderful play of light and shadows occurs, imparting movement and life to the space. Shelves around the room hold treasured objects and photographs and a single neon band frames the ceiling where daylight enters. The simple plan and minimal detailing of the interior space reinforce the importance of the personal mementos and furnishings, including furniture from the client's family home. A love for contemporary art, as well as her own pursuits as an artist, are integral to the design.

A trellis extends out at a point just above the full height of the windows, creating a framework for colorful flowers and vines.

Sitting on top of the addition is a copper-clad sun scoop. The copper fins of the scoop refer to a sculpture of swimming fish that appears on an adjacent roof. The sun scoop brings morning sun into the west-facing room, enabling light to fill the space throughout the day. Small panes of glass form window walls on two sides of the room, recalling the glassed-in porch of her childhood. A series of steel-angles affixed to the outside of the box align with the horizontal window mullions and find their counterpoints in the steel trellis overhead. The trellis extends out at a point just above the full height of the windows, creating a framework for growing colorful flowers and vines.

Left:
The sun scoop brings morning sun into the west-facing room, enabling light to fill the space throughout the day. Shelves around the room hold treasured objects and photographs intended to promote healing reflection and memory for one suffering from Alzheimer's disease.

Facing page:
Floating in the treetops, the Memory Room captures the feel of a tree house.

All photos: Michael Jensen
All plans and drawins: Olson Sundberg Architects

The Memory Room addition takes
the form of a box projecting away
from the main body of the house
and floats over the ravine below.

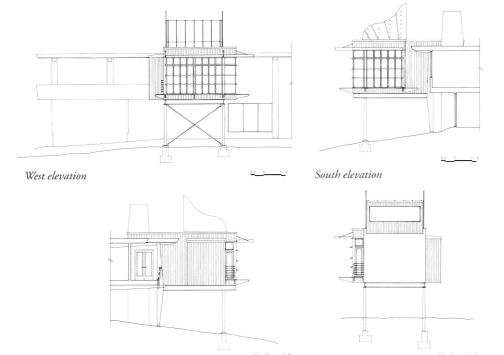

West elevation

South elevation

North sectional elevation

East sectional elevation

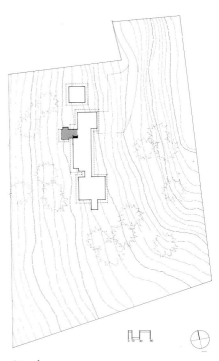

Site plan

Throughout the day, a wonderful play of light and shadows occurs,
imparting movement and life to the space.

Hauptman House

FAIRFIELD, IOWA

At the center of the plan, the Brahmasthan offers a space with no active function, creating a silent hub that ties together the active rooms of the house.
Photos: Anthony Lawlor

Set amid the cornfields of Iowa, the Hauptman home draws upon the 5,000-year-old East Indian building science of Maharishi Sthapatya-Ved to enhance a contemporary lifestyle. The name *Sthapatya-Ved* comes from the Sanskrit roots *sthapana,* to establish, and *veda,* knowledge. This method of design, therefore, seeks to establish dwelling places where the inhabitants use knowledge of the laws of nature to gain increased balance, harmony, and well-being.

The 6,500-square-foot (604-square-meter) home employs several devices to achieve these goals. The symmetrical floor plan is oriented to the cardinal directions, attuning the home to the regular cycles of the sun's daily and seasonal path over the landscape. At the center of the plan, the Brahmasthan is a space that does not have an active function, creating a silent hub that ties together the active rooms of the house. This peaceful core allows one to sense the wholeness of the structure at all times and minimizes experiences of fragmentation and isolation. At the perimeter of the plan, a colonnade porch mediates the relationship between interior and exterior, forming a zone of transition that weaves the shapes, textures, colors, and smells of nature into the human-made realm.

Each room of the house is positioned to receive a particular quality of energy produced by the sun to enhance the activity performed in that room. Quiet rooms, for example, are oriented toward the tranquil morning light; active rooms open to the more excited light of midday and afternoon. The entrance faces east to receive the renewing rays of dawn. The east elevation employs temple-like elements to honor this relationship. Natural materials are used throughout to provide a toxin-free environment and bring the textures and colors of nature into the home.

The Hauptman home creates a haven of peace and renewal where body, mind, and spirit can be restored and nourished by the forces that invigorate life on earth.

At the perimeter of the plan, a colonnade porch mediates the relationship between interior and exterior, forming a zone of overlap that weaves the shapes, textures, colors, and smells of nature into the human-made realm.

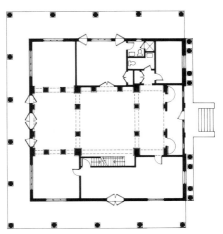

Floor plan:
The simple geometry and precise orientation of the symmetrical floor plan attune the house to the regular cycles of the sun's daily and seasonal path.

Credit: Anthony Lawlor Architect

The colonnade porch offers a quiet place from which to observe the surrounding landscape. Photos, this page: Anthony Lawlor

A colonnade porch wraps around three sides of the house, creating a transition zone between interior and exterior.

The quiet rooms are oriented toward the tranquil morning light and active rooms open to the more vivid light of midday and afternoon.
Photos, top and bottom right: Anthony Lawlor

The bedrooms, considered quiet rooms, are oriented to capture the rejuvenating rays of the morning sun.
Photo: Rick Donhauser

A silent hub ties together the active rooms of the house. Natural materials are used throughout to provide a toxin-free environment and bring the textures and colors of nature into the home.

Pawson Residence

LONDON, ENGLAND

An elegant compressed staircase leads to the second floor.
Photos: Todd Eberle

The facade of this existing Victorian house in west London remains virtually unchanged except for a new recessed entry. The original interiors were removed and replaced with new floorboards, white walls, and white ceilings. Unwanted materials were subtracted to enable the specific material of the project to emerge uninhibited. As a result, the feeling produced by these specific materials, in combination with and in relation to other materials, is one of wonder and sensual delight.

The raised ground-floor entry opens to a large space with two fireplaces that were retained from the two original reception rooms. A deep structural member remains to delineate the imprint of what was two spaces. A simple stone bench on the long wall functions as hearth, seating, and source of light. The only furnishings are a table, stools, and two chairs made of oak. A row of pivoting doors conceals storage on the opposite wall. Uncut wood floorboards are laid from the front of the house to the back and extend outside to become the garden balcony. The galley kitchen has two white marble work surfaces. A balcony off the kitchen leads to the Garden Room, a spatial extension of the interior, with stone floor, table, and stools. A simple trellis encloses this room on three sides.

A set of straight wood stairs leads to the second-level bathroom, where a wash basin and bath are carved out of hewn stone. Gaps in the paved floor accommodate water that brims over from the tub. The two children's rooms occupy the same floor with beds, shelves, and desks built of the same wood. The top floor abounds with natural light and contains the main bedroom.

The lack of hardware, moldings, and other clutter throughout the space highlights the effect of specific material selections and elegant proportions. The rich palette of materials consists of Douglas fir floorboards 45 feet (13.5 meters) long and 18 inches (45.5 centimeters) wide; Carrara marble counter tops 4 inches (10 centimeters) thick and 14 feet (4.5 meters) long; a wash basin and bath carved out of hewn stone; doors with no visible hinges or knobs; and door frames with concealed switch-plates. The large scale of materials used is experienced as temporal weight when one's body comes in contact with them, reading the interior structure, or applying a heavy touch.

The selection and use of materials goes beyond the visual and embraces the tactile. Carrara marble is used because its luminosity and visual depth reflect a desire for a haptic rather than a merely optic visual expression. Pawson talks about his home as a place where he experiences that haptic visual pleasure, creating a state he refers to as "visual calm."

All plans and drawings: John Pawson Architect

The Garden Room functions as a spatial extension of the interior, with stone floor, wood table, and two stools.

The entrance to the house opens into a large room where a simple stone bench on the long wall functions as hearth, seating, and source of light. The only furnishings are a table and two chairs made of wood.

Floor plans

The wash basin and bath are carved out of hewn stone. Gaps in the paved floor accommodate water that brims over from the tub.
Photo: Todd Eberle

Stone steps lead to the garden room. Pawson states, "A town garden is a paradise, an enclosed private place."
Photo: Richard Glover

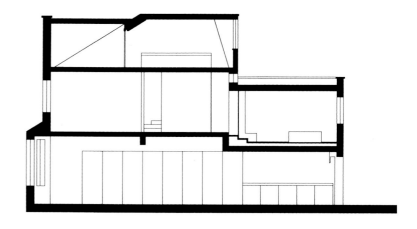

Building section

The galley kitchen has two white Carrara marble counter tops, 4 inches (10 centimeters) thick and 14 feet (4.5 meters) long. Pawson uses Carrara marble for its luminosity and visual depth.
Photos, this page: Todd Eberle

Douglas fir floorboards run the length of the house from front to back, and simple furniture, a table, stools, and two chairs of oak, occupy the main living space.

Industrial/Corporate Spaces

Historically, the relationship between Western culture and industry has been one of ambivalence. The effort to transcend the division of labor and the hard realities of industrial production resulted in a fluctuation between two perceptual extremes. On one hand, industry was viewed as the necessary source of cultural prosperity, yet there existed a level of denial regarding machine-production environments. As a building type, the factory was a machine for production and the factory worker merely a cog in its wheel. Factory design reflected this viewpoint and responded to the needs of productivity and efficiency. The impact was critical, as working people found themselves without a voice and disenfranchised victims of poor working environments. Employers found themselves confronting issues of absenteeism, turnover, and low morale as well as shifts in productivity. The connection between productivity and working conditions had not yet been made.

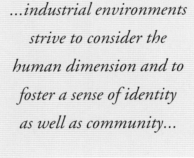

...industrial environments strive to consider the human dimension and to foster a sense of identity as well as community...

The idea that increased productivity and employee satisfaction go hand in hand as a result of a sustaining work environment is accepted among most industrialists today. After World War II, the industrial building type received much scrutiny in Europe and North America, due to advances in technology and the reemergence of labor unions. New technology brought the individualized machine shifting the emphasis from long assembly lines to large, open production floors. Unions, in advocating for factory workers, pushed for humanizing conditions such as natural light and views, auditory controls, and ventilation.

J. Irwin Miller, who launched the quantity of good building in Columbus, Indiana, was instrumental in bringing enhanced design awareness to the postwar American work environment. He was a leader in establishing a precedent for quality building design and emphasized its relationship to its users. His love and concern for the people of his hometown was expressed through the architecture that was commissioned, with the factory setting being no exception. He believed that a quality environment exerts a positive force on people's lives and, ultimately, on their ability to arrive at and understand the concept of excellence.

Today, more industrial environments strive to consider the human dimension and to foster a sense of identity as well as community. The division of labor appears less obvious as the functional boundaries between office and production worker are blurred. Working conditions have made significant leaps; many designed environments include an abundance of natural light and views, fitness centers, common meeting areas, artwork, indoor gardens, and outdoor recreation areas. Our attitude has changed to acknowledge the importance of industrial production within global culture. Comprehensive designs that have a deeper knowledge of industrial production and working conditions foster and perpetuate an egalitarian sense of community within those environments.

Left:
A night view of the Miller SQA Factory, Holland, Michigan, stretched along a low ridge, captures its subtle integration with the natural landscape.
Photos: Timothy Hursley

Facing page:
Natural light is brought into the production areas of the Miller SQA Factory through exterior windows, skylights, and as borrowed light from the interior "street."

Exxon Company USA
Brookhollow Campus
Heart of the Campus
HOUSTON, TEXAS

Koi, waterlilies, and horsetail add interest to the pool. The small bubblers provide sound and ripple the water surface.
Photos, this page: The Office of James Burnett

The stones are set in crushed gravel as they cross the slate dining terrace. Douglas fir arbors are shaped to repeat the campus canopy system. Drake elms extended from trays of yellow flag iris provide filtered light. The warm tones of the arbor, stone, and planting make these terraces comfortable and relaxing.

Exxon Brookhollow is a suburban office complex built in the 1970s as a single-tenant campus for 1,500 employees. In early 1996, Exxon decided to renovate the cafeteria and include an exterior garden as part of that plan. Flanked by buildings on all sides, this 1/2-acre (.2-hectare) garden was given the name Heart of the Campus for its proximity and importance. The intention was to create a place of refuge from the surrounding office environment, offering maximum flexibility for communion, reflection, and celebration.

The Heart of the Campus is designed as a series of appropriately scaled garden rooms subtly defined by plantings of ornamental grasses, perennials, and herbs. The center piece of the garden is a 14 by 65-foot (4.5 by 20-meter) lily and koi pool, which is divided at two locations with steppingstones. The koi add a layer of richness and interest to the living pool through their perpetual dance. Teak benches flank the pool, separated from the water by narrow bands of lawn and crushed stone, while Drake elms and flowering hedge bars define the court.

The dining terraces, adjacent to the center court, are designed with matching bosques of Drake elms, separated by Douglas fir arbors, which provide a pleasant shade. The heavy beam arbors are covered with flowering, fragrant wisteria and are shaped to complement the campuswide canopy system. The terraces offer a sense of enclosure while providing a filtered view of both the center court and the herb garden. The kitchen/herb beds were designed to offer year-round seasonal interest through their color, texture, and scent. Visitors are fascinated by the production and harvest of the herbs, coordinated by the herb gardener and chef for daily use in the kitchen.

A small grove of oaks and pines was preserved at the east end of the center court. A large raised wood deck was constructed with carve-outs for important specimen trees. This area offers the most moderate microclimate within the garden, and is used year round for meetings, dining, and special occasions. The north boundary of the Heart of the Campus is the 40 by 160-foot (12 by 49-meter) wall of the central plant. It was painted by a muralist as a series of four floral images reminiscent of the series of garden rooms that make up this restorative exterior environment.

The dining terrace is shaded with Drake elms and Douglas fir arbors.
Filtered views are available to the center court and the kitchen/herb garden.
The movable furniture makes this terrace a popular gathering place.
Photo: Jim Wilson

The pool is crossed with oversized rough-cut steppingstones at two locations. The 4-foot (1-meter) shelf in the center of the pool is designed to offer relief for the koi as well as visual interest from above.
Photo: Jim Wilson

The rough-cut stones pass through the slate dining terrace and cross the pool at two locations, encouraging people to interact with the koi. The daily feeding for the fish is handled by the visitors.
Photos, left and below:
The Office of James Burnett

Mexican beach pebbles and horsetail make an interesting textural composition along the glass wall of the cafe.

*The woodland deck provides the Heart of the Campus with a cool, shady,
and somewhat private outdoor room overlooking the center-court garden.
Photo: Jim Wilson*

A wall of the central plant building, measuring 40' x 160' (12 x 49 meters), is used as a painted canvas for one edge of the garden. Rows of ornamental grasses and flowering perennials bordered with gravel bands make the foreground for this mural.
Photos, this page:
The Office of James Burnett

This view across the pool to the cafe illustrates the stones apparently floating just above the surface of the water.

Purple sage, Mexican mint marigold, and lemongrass are among the plants that make up the kitchen/herb garden areas. These gardens are designed for sensory stimulation through their fragrance, color, and edible qualities. Photo: Jim Wilson

Miller SQA Factory

HOLLAND, MICHIGAN

Nestled along a low ridge of prairie grasses in western Michigan, Miller SQA, a subsidiary of furniture maker Herman Miller, Inc., is a 295,000-square-foot (27,405.5-square-meter) office, manufacturing, and distribution center. Herman Miller's corporate culture has long prided itself on well-designed products, egalitarian ideals, and a strong sensitivity to how their buildings look and function, and Miller SQA is no exception.

The company has a history of conservation, recycling, and regard for the work environment. A team of design specialists brought together in the early stages of development ensured that these ideals were shared and perpetuated throughout the process. A single-story,

The building is surrounded by a "living landscape" of mixed grasses and wild flowers. Constructed wetlands were created to filter storm water runoff.

All photos: Timothy Hursley
All plans and drawings: William McDonough + Partners

crescent-shaped structure that follows the natural contours of the site is the result of this effort. The landscape design demonstrates sensitivity to the natural surroundings and minimizes the environmental consequences of the building.

A day-lit interior "street" functions as the spine of the building, uniting a low band of offices at the front with the high-production block at the rear. Effective placement of shared resources, including photocopy and conference areas, a cafeteria, and a fitness center, allows interaction between office and factory workers. Interior courtyards and outdoor planted areas within the same vicinity provide a relaxing area for work breaks. The entire building is brightly lit, with roof monitors, skylights, and sloped glazing. To reduce energy consumption, photosensors monitor the use of artificial light and operable windows in office areas provide an abundance of fresh air and views.

The main entry opens to views of the natural landscape with the high-production block beyond raised to capture maximum daylight.

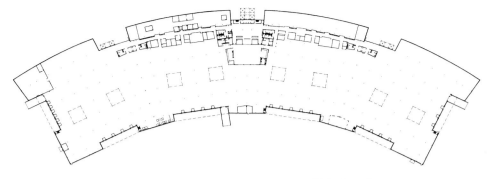

Main floor plan

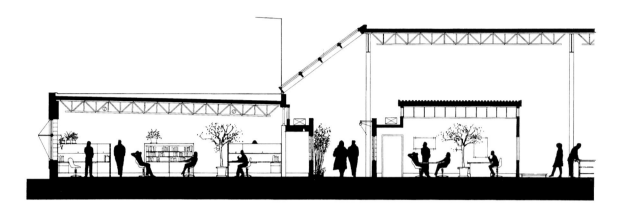

Building section through offices and interior "street."

Natural light is brought into the production areas through exterior windows, skylights, and as borrowed light from the interior "street."

Overhead glazing supplies the landscaped interior "street" and offices with abundant daylight.

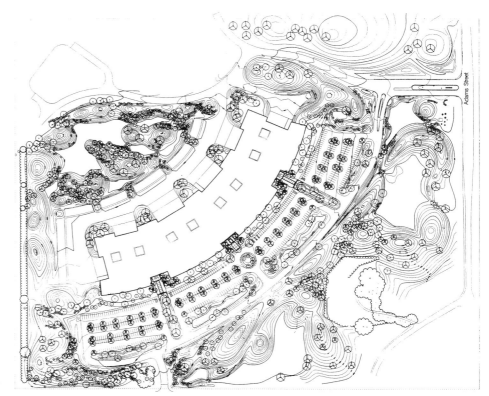

Site Plan

*A night view of the building, stretched along a low ridge,
captures its subtle integration with the natural landscape.*

The day-lit interior "street" provides opportunity for chance encounters between office and factory workers.

The Body Shop Canada Home Office

DON MILLS, ONTARIO, CANADA

One of the key aspects of the facility is the Living Machine, a unique biological waste-water treatment system, one of the first in Canada. It is located in a 4,000-square-foot (372 square-meter) greenhouse that also acts as a Trombe wall, providing insulation for the building.

All photos: David Whittaker

"Be bold. Be daring. Be different. Be caring." This is the unique business philosophy of The Body Shop Canada. Committed to "profits with principles," The Body Shop is renowned for its innovative approach to retailing and its unyielding commitment to environmental, social, and corporate responsibility. The new facility is the embodiment of the company's distinct corporate culture.

The Body Shop Canada embodies innovative building, landscape design, and technological advances in engineering, energy conservation and waste management. The intent was to design a supportive work environment that was affordable and easy for other corporations to emulate. The building, once a printing plant, successfully and creatively integrated recycled and reclaimed materials and earth-friendly finishes. The Living Machine, a unique biological waste-water treatment system, one of the first in Canada, is housed in a 4,000-square-foot (372 square-meter) greenhouse that also acts as a Trombe wall, providing insulation for the building. The landscape architecture includes a physic garden, designed as a teaching environment, to educate employees about the medicinal qualities of the plants and herbs used in their company's products.

Designed as a mini-city, the facility encourages spontaneous contact and interaction between people throughout the workplace. A circular hub acts as a meeting place and action center for environmental and social campaigns the company is working on. The best space in the building, because of its views to the surrounding landscape and maximum amounts of daylight, is given to the on-site day-care center. The use of natural light was critical to the design of the open, people-friendly work environment. The building design enables people who spend most of the workday at a desk to have the maximum amount of light, while skylights and glass walls bring light into the building interior.

The Body Shop Canada takes a holistic approach to providing an enjoyable, supportive, people-oriented workplace. The day-lit lobby features a mini-shop where products are displayed and a large window opens to the bottle-filling area, enabling people to witness the cycle of business.

The facility is designed like a mini-city, with main halls or "avenues" leading out from Inspiration Intersection to the different "neighborhood" work areas, each with a distinct identity, color scheme, and layout.

The Body Shop Canada is designed to encourage spontaneous contact and interaction among employees. A circular hub, Inspiration
Intersection, acts as a meeting place and displays information on
the company's numerous projects, including new products and
environmental and social campaigns.

The Department of the Future, The Body Shop's on-site day-care center, has views to the surrounding landscape and provides parents from the Body Shop Home Office and the community a safe, enjoyable, inexpensive place to leave their children while they are at work.

The building's open-style cafeteria and meeting area, designed in many ways to be homelike, includes a kitchen, a fireplace, and access to an exterior patio and landscaped gardens.

The Bored Room features reclaimed and refurbished furniture as well as a window to the production floor, thus placing staff face to face with the core of The Body Shop's success—its products.

QMR Plastics Facility

RIVER FALLS, WISCONSIN

There is a new understanding that people don't just work for money. The workplace is a hotbed for human connections, and making that space comfortable, usable, and productive is what architecture is challenged to do.

Julie Snow

The Quadion Minnesota Rubber (QMR) facility is located in the rolling farmland and glaciated till of western Wisconsin. Surrounded by a wooded ridge on the south and west, the facility forms a transition between the agricultural lands and the town nearby. The 10-acre (4-hectare) site, a runoff retention pond, and the use of native prairie grasses and flowers mitigate the effects of construction on the land.

QMR's success depends on its ability to attract and keep conscientious and well-trained staff. The design of a facility demonstrates corporate investment in employees' well-being. Daylight, structure and skin, and the spatial organization transform this building from one that efficiently houses manufacturing equipment to one that carefully considers the experience of the production worker.

Light modulates the workday through the movement of light, shade, and shadow across the building and as the angle of sun changes throughout the day and the year. On the protected south facade, the glass extends from the concrete slab to the steel deck, offering direct experience of the wooded hill from the production area. Working with machines all day amplifies the human need for connection and shared purpose. The openness of the facility and its layers of transparency allow a sense of that connection throughout the entire building. The employee lunchroom is located to enable direct observation of the daily and seasonal changes of the prairie and forested hill.

The worker's experience also requires that the architecture support efficient and convenient job performance. Preengineered trusses and tilt-up precast concrete provide a production space 20 feet (6 meters) clear to the bottom of structure with a clear span of 90 feet (27.5 meters), allowing for the easy operation of equipment. Access to power, cooling, and air is provided at intervals by service pedestals connected to central services by tunnels below the slab. The production floor is cleared of all piping to presses, creating an uninterrupted and clean work space.

Overlooked by a wooded ridge on the south and west, the facility forms a transition from the agricultural lands and the town nearby.

All photos: Don Wong

Facing page:
The employee lunchroom is located to enable direct observation of the daily and seasonal changes of the prairie and forested hill.

On the protected south facade, the glass extends from the concrete slab to the steel deck, offering the direct experience of the wooded hill from the production area.

The openness of the facility and layers of transparency allow a sense of connection throughout the entire building.

Administrative areas are strongly linked to the surrounding environment and enjoy an abundance of natural light.

Precast concrete panels, colored to reflect the limestone rock revealed in nearby roadcuts, anchor the building in the site. Dormers along the roof form a reverse cant, suggesting a horizontal roof line.

Outer Circle Products Offices

CHICAGO, ILLINOIS

The new facade is made from the same raw steel and cast glass used in the surrounding buildings in a reference to the history of Chicago's industrial building materials.
Photo: Mike Suomi

In a time when many businesses are moving to the suburbs, Outer Circle Products made a conscious choice to remain in Chicago and to give back to this working city through employment opportunities and thoughtful rebuilding. Located on the bank of the north branch of the Chicago River, the facility includes a new shipping and receiving center and the adaptive reconstruction of two contiguous masonry and heavy-timber structures used for office and factory space. The owner wanted an environment that challenged people, encouraged interaction, and fostered change and evolution. The central concept involved breaking down the hierarchy and subsequent barriers that typically exist between labor and management and between management divisions. Great efforts were made to salvage and reuse materials and preserve the beauty of the existing building in this low-budget design, which includes custom furniture, signage, lighting, and hardware designed and fabricated by the architect. The design for the shipping and receiving building celebrates Chicago's heritage as a working city, utilizing traditional industrial materials painted in colors suggestive of the companys products.

Employee experience and perception was critical to the success of the design, as was the interactive and democratic design-review process. Six departments on two levels were organized as "neighborhoods" to reflect a sense of small communities within the company. Workspaces are arranged around four open "squares," encouraging spontaneous interaction and meeting. The neighborhoods open to a central, two-story atrium "town square," which organizes public functions such as message board, copy, fax, conference rooms, and primary circulation, tying the space together horizontally and vertically. The cafeteria resembles a restaurant with custom tables, chairs, and light fixtures, and demonstrates the company's commitment to providing a sustaining environment for its employees. Great effort was made to achieve home-like levels of comfort throughout the facility through the use of materials, lighting, and color. Special attention was paid to eye-level details and tactile elements that people continually engage throughout their workday, including chairs, desks, doors, hardware, and signage.

Consistent with the palette of materials used on the interior, the new warehouse addition uses raw and corrugated steel and masonry and reflects the "big shoulders" of the worker.
Photos, above and facing: David Clifton

Facing page:
A custom steel stair and conference tower are the focal points of the two-story sky-lit atrium space housing the production line at the heart of the facility. A large clock looms overhead and an LCD screen displays production figures and messages for the workers.

The architect designed and fabricated special eye-level details and tactile elements that people engage throughout their work-day, including chairs, desks, doors, hardware, and signage.
Photos: Mike Suomi

A third-floor office "neighborhood," with custom column lamps made from old World War II bomb-shells, light coves, and workstations arranged around an open "square," encourages spontaneous interaction and meeting.

Office "neighborhoods" are organized around and open to a central two-story atrium "town square" and reflect a sense of small communities within the company. Visitors must walk through the production area to reach the offices.

Photos: David Clifton

The grand staircase in the two-story sky-lit atrium leads to the
production floor from the offices on the second and third levels.
The conference tower beyond serves as shared meeting space and
is the only enclosed area in the facility.

Memorials and Public Spaces

There exists an essential and universal need for public urban space. Cities of every age have made provisions for open places to promote social encounters and collective civic affairs. Throughout time, the public place has been a destination for ritual and interaction that we are all free to occupy, either as an active participant or a passive observer. The mere fact that a public realm exists is testimony to our emotional and psychological need to periodically rediscover our link to the larger community.

How and why people gather in public space reflects a continuous evolution that mirrors the culture and its social and economic conditions. Who gathers has evolved to embody a composite of constantly shifting and overlapping groups. Today, encounters with traditional public space have become increasingly superfluous, as we seek the more insular, privatized public environments of shopping malls, theme parks, and atrium spaces. However, we still want to be with other people in an environment that connects us with new sensations, new people, and new ideas; and we still want the opportunity to be interactive and participate in those environments—however briefly and noncommittally, whether actively or passively.

> *A public space that unites us all, pulling us to run our fingers across a surface, listen to a trickle of water, gaze into a reflection, or simply stand, the contemporary memorial examines our need for contemplation and depth.*

The memorial, as a realm of public space, offers a more intimate public connection in the preservation of an experience that is in some way shared. Over time, memorials have evolved to be less about an object in the environment and more about creating holistic settings for the acknowledgment of strong and complicated feelings. Memorials today have a seemingly gentler connotation and a more personal communication with the viewer than those of yesteryear. A public space that unites us all, pulling us to run our fingers across a surface, listen to a trickle of water, gaze into a reflection, or simply stand, the contemporary memorial examines our need for contemplation and depth. It challenges us with the task of keeping our values and aspirations aligned with our wishes and needs, acting to counter the expedience that dominates our daily lives.

Contemporary public places have little semblance of history or shared community spirit. The rituals of social interaction have changed the profile of public space, weaving a landscape of more private realms, yet our need to gather, to discover one another, and to participate in the public realm is very real. Public spaces are crucial as environments where we come together for shared and private experience—a sequence of perceptions, sensations, emotions, and value—linking us to a larger sense of time and place.

Left:
Kobe Nishiokamoto Housing, Kobe, Japan.
Photo: Timothy Hursley

Facing page:
Meditation Space, UNESCO Headquarters, Paris, France.
Photo: Stephan Couturier

Oklahoma City Memorial

OKLAHOMA CITY, OKLAHOMA

We come here to remember those who were killed, those who survived, and those who were changed forever. May all who leave here know the impact of violence. May this memorial offer comfort, strength, peace, hope, and serenity.

Memorial Mission Statement

The Oklahoma City Memorial resembles a large outdoor room in which zones of space provide opportunities for intimate contemplation, enabling each visitor to find a place that corresponds to their stage in the healing process. Access to the site occurs through buffer zones on the north, east, and west. To the north, an orchard of fruit trees filters dust and noise, and to the east and west, formal overscaled entry gates lead visitors into the site. The gates are filters as well, similar to Native American dream catchers, screening evil spirits and allowing only good spirits to pass through to the sacred grounds.

The design of the complex represents the juxtaposition of two fates. To the south, on the footprint of the former Murrah Building, now a sloping grass field, 168 empty glass-based chairs are placed in memory of those who died. At night the chairs are illuminated and become beacons of hope. Evergreen trees surround the building site as if to watch over the chairs, providing a protected area to walk quietly. Directly north, across a shallow reflecting pool, a series of terraces rise up to the Survivor Tree, witness to the violence of the moment, commemorating strength and endurance. The terraces offer places to pause and reflect, looking back across the field of empty chairs. The fruit orchard that surrounds the Survivor Tree offers a canopy of shade and scent. An area for children in a clearing amid the orchard provides an opportunity for them to learn, interact, and express their feelings. Again and again, the visitor is encouraged to confront tragedy and consider its meaning in their own lives and in the life of their community and nation.

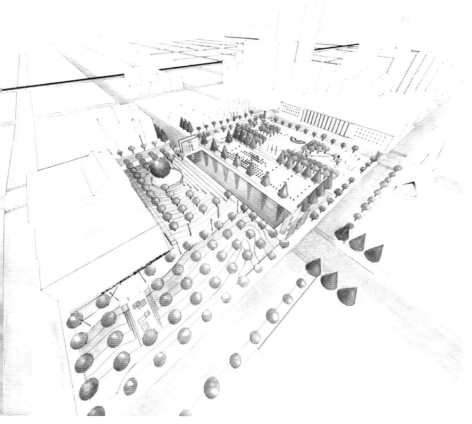

A bird's-eye perspective demonstrating how the memorial is integrated with the surrounding downtown area. The design attempts to unify the events of April 19, 1995, with its place and community.

All drawings and models: Butzer Design Partnership

*A night image viewed from the Survivor Tree captures the warm glow
of the 168 chairs as day moves into night.*

A perspective looking south from the memorial museum's corner window to the memorial site reveals high tree canopies and well-lit paths that ensure easy orientation and safety, day and night.

The perspective shows the strong relationship of the children's area to the museum's lobby. Teachers and museum guides instruct school groups in both in-door and outdoor learning activity areas.

A perspective of the reflecting pool's edge, where visitors may gather to witness how a city has overcome tragedy through unity.

Facing page:
Site plan

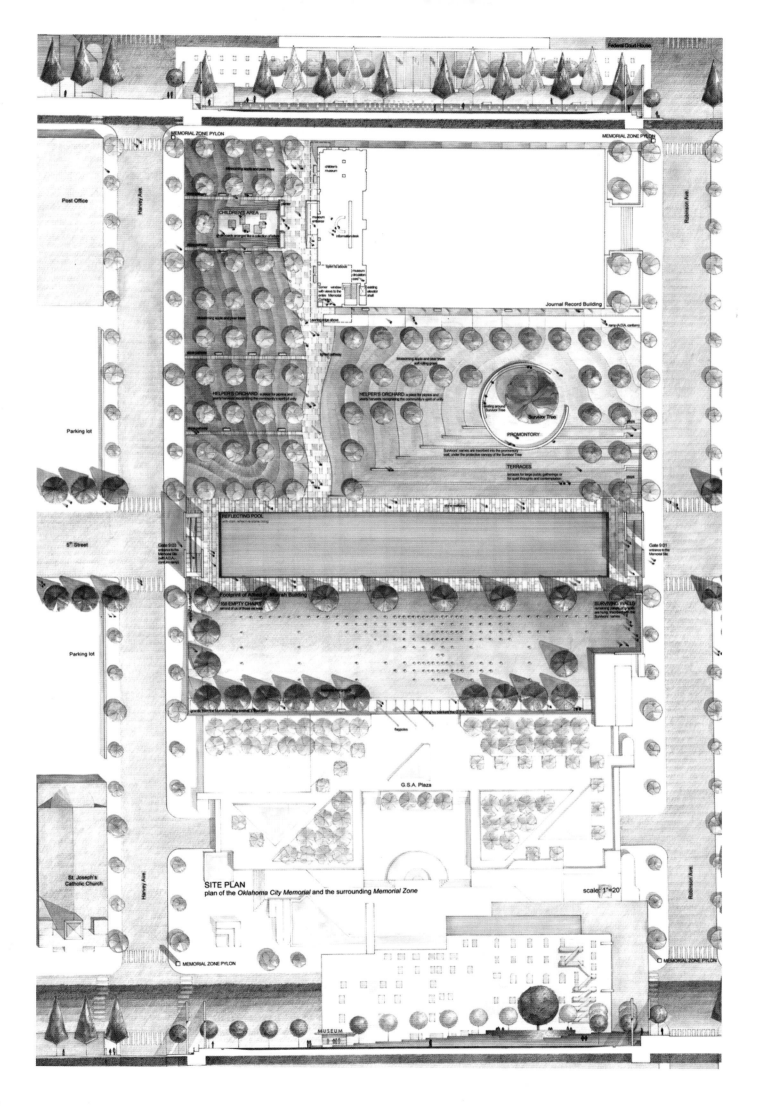

SITE PLAN
plan of the *Oklahoma City Memorial* and the surrounding *Memorial Zone*

scale: 1"=20'

Avenue Number 5
World Expo

SEVILLE, SPAIN

This public space project is one of five main pedestrian corridors providing access to the national pavilions at the Seville World Expo '92. The concept is designed as a narrative experience; it celebrates the river city of Seville and its history as a route to the sea for fifteenth-century explorers, the general Expo theme of discovery, and the technological emphasis of the fair.

Consistent with the river image, the west part of Avenue Number 5 represents the source of the water in the mountains, the center is the river itself, and the east end suggests the exit to the sea. This effect is achieved by an undulating wall of water and glass 328 yards (300 meters) long and 6.5 yards (6 meters) high running the length of the avenue. Covered by an elevated landscape, all of the restaurant facilities and the monorail station are enclosed within the water wall, and each is shaded by either lifted vegetation and trees or a vine-covered trellis.

Great historic environments have taught us that people relate favorably to a space in proportion to the respect it shows for their physical stature and sense of well-being. The use of intriguing visual features is essential and is captured in this expansive water wall. Equally important are elements that relate to body perception and multisensory experience, resulting in an environment that one can move through and interact with as well as hear, smell, taste, and touch. In this environment, visitors feel inspired to invent relationships with others and with the physical and aesthetic elements of the design.

A key element in the development of dynamic public space today is a sensitivity to the new world of integrated systems, based on models found in nature. From a visual perspective, this calls for the development of images that reflect the spirit of multimedia communications, combined with the earth awareness of resource conservation. It is a way of working that involves the seamless fusion of art, architecture, and context; calling for a kind of strong interdisciplinary commitment from outside the project, resulting in public spaces where it becomes impossible to discern where one art form begins and the other ends.

James Wines, SITE

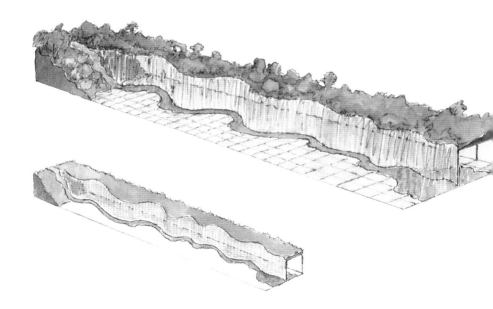

Concept drawing

All photos and drawings: SITE Environmental Design

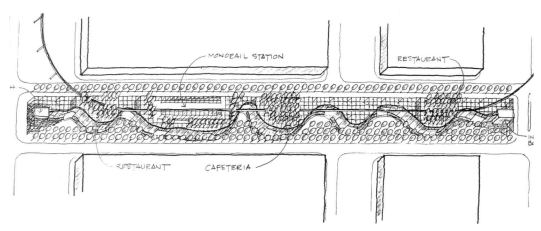

Conceptual site plan

The curvilinear plaza steps serve as terraces and lead down to a shallow pool and an undulating water wall.

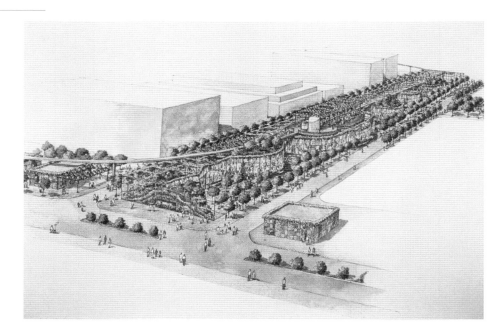

Conceptual drawings of curving waterfall

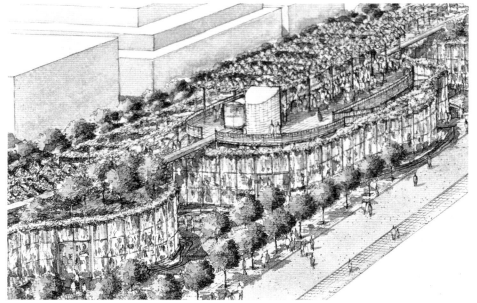

The blurred image of children sitting in one of the garden areas, as seen through the waterwall.

The undulating waterwall takes on a different character at night when lit at night by a fireworks display in the background.

The curving waterwall reflects the "inside-outside" relationship of the surrounding trees and the adjacent restaurant's interior vegetation.

The deep shade provided by the pergolas and "growing" colonnade offers protection from the elements yet does not inhibit views. Street-level observation is critical to creating appropriate scale in a planned civic environment.

Children play in the waterwall, demonstrating the value of creating an environment where one can experience the design with all the senses— touch, smell, taste, hearing, and sight.

The grand processional features vine-covered pergolas and a "growing" colonnade. This "art as climate control" concept is created by placing seeded earth in perforated metal cylinders.

Gardens, Kobe Nishiokamoto Housing
KOBE, JAPAN

Site perspective
Site plan: Moore Ruble Yudell

At the foot of the Rokko Mountain range, this 9-acre (3.5-hectare), 300-unit housing project addresses a number of contemporary challenges that face the master planning and design of large urban spaces. Issues of individual and community identity, human scale, connection to nature, and placemaking were all critical to the success of the project. The site had been poorly developed in the 1950s, destroying its natural topography and amenities. A great deal of time was spent to restore and capture the site's inherent special properties. Of significance was its location between the mountains and the sea and the discovery of a natural spring when the land was restored to its original topography.

Building on the essential elements of the site, the master plan reflects the intersection of two paths: a formal axis of courtyards relating to the city and an informal axis of gardens relating to the topography. The informal axis begins with a mountain garden containing a natural spring that feeds downslope through a meadow garden and on to an ocean garden. The formal axis begins with a elliptical entry courtyard, steps down to a courtyard with allées of magnolias, and continues on to an axial view of the mountains. The two axes meet at the serpentine garden, resolving the two geometries and expressing the harmony of the yin-yang relationship.

The buildings are carefully shaped to define positive open spaces whose shape and scale is coherent. They also step from three stories to eleven, framing views and creating profiles that connect to the hills beyond. The courtyards and gardens are a narrative to be experienced individually or as a continuous journey. The harmony between the buildings and the gardens creates a sense of peace without denying the energy of urban living. The result is a humane environment where people do not have to flee the city to experience the natural world.

The elliptical entry court creates a quiet transitional zone as one moves form the intense traffic of the neighborhood to the central lobby and arrival of the project.
Photo: Timothy Hursley

A rock wall of both dressed and natural stone creates a transition from the formality of the large building to the more informally composed meadow garden.
Photos, above and below left:
Moore Ruble Yudell

A pavilion at the mountain garden suggests the integration of nature with the geometries of the built environment.

The central reflecting pool of the formal garden draws the eye from the lobby to the garden and on toward the mountains.
Photo: Timothy Hursley

A finely honed stone fountain creates a quiet but mesmerizing sheet of water.
Photo: T. Hanawa

The largest apartment tower uses changes in material, texture, and proportion to scale down to the intimacy of the garden.
Photo: Timothy Hursley

The formal garden, flanked by large buildings, is parsed into intimate seating spaces where formal landscape creates both a link and a complement to the architecture.
Photo: T. Hanawa

The elliptical entry court organizes formal planting in rhythmic relation to the architecture, thus reinforcing the strong link between the architecture and the landscape.
Photo: Moore Ruble Yudell

The introduction of iridescent tiles lets simple planes of water sparkle in kaleidoscopic reflections.
Photo: T. Hanawa

Passage between two courtyards occurs through an arcade, behind a sparkling waterfall. Sound and light subtly animate this place of movement and contemplation.
Photo: T. Hanawa

Meditation Space
UNESCO Headquarters
PARIS, FRANCE

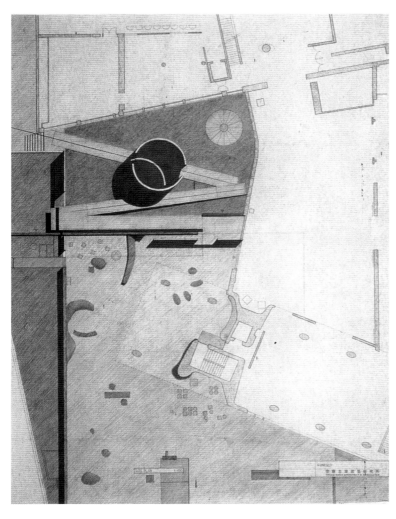

Drawing of site

The United Nations Educational Scientific Cultural Organization (UNESCO) was established at the end of World War II with the purpose of contributing to the establishment of world peace through the promotion of education, science, and culture. In 1995, UNESCO celebrated its fiftieth anniversary and in honor of this occasion, Director-General Frederico Mayor suggested that a meditation space be constructed on the site of UNESCO Headquarters in Paris.

The UNESCO headquarters was designed by Marcel Breuer; the site includes a Japanese garden designed by Isamu Noguchi. Both projects created a significant context for the meditation space and were honored throughout the design process. The meditation space is a single-story cylindrical reinforced-concrete structure surrounded by a shallow pool of water. Unfinished concrete walls, marked only by traces of function, enclose the space. Simple cut openings receive the ramped walkway that intersects the space and moves people through the site above a shallow plane of water. A narrow slot opening surrounds the ceiling perimeter, allowing light to wash the walls and impart movement to the room, as well as giving a weightlessness to the ceiling plane. Granite that was exposed to radiation from the atomic bomb at Hiroshima is used in a radial pattern on the floor and for the base of the pool. The site is approximately 3,900 square feet (362.5 square meters), the building occupying a floor area of 370 square feet (34.5 square meters) and a height of 21 feet (6.5 meters).

Designed as a place of prayer for eternal world peace, the meditation space embraces all people, transcending their religious, ethical, cultural, and historical differences and conflicts. In keeping with its function and purpose, the space appears serene and solemn. The simplicity of form, homogeneous use of material, neutral tone, and the subtle use of light and shadow create an environment that relates not only to sight but to the other senses as well, establishing a perceptual stage upon which the body moves and interacts. The silent intensity held within this finely crafted concrete form offers strength and power in the quest for global peace.

All plans and drawings: Tadao Ando Architect and Associates

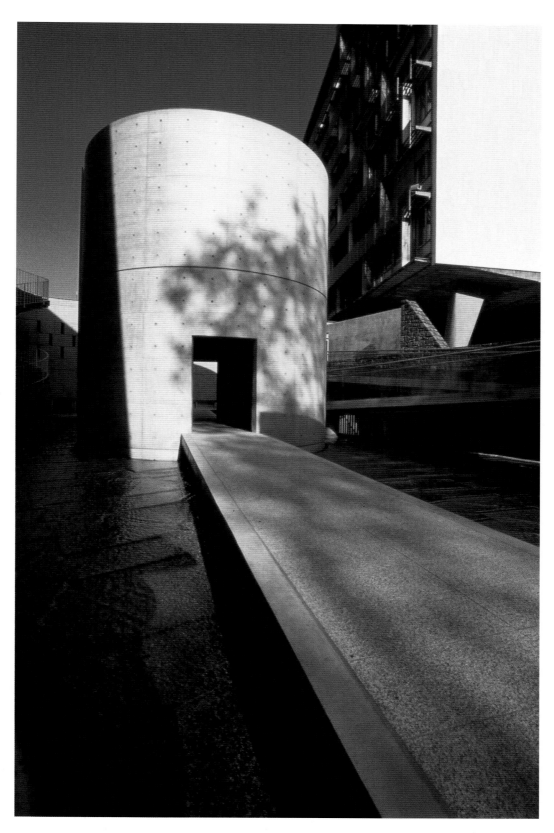

*A concrete walkway to the meditation space
overlooks a pool of water. The base of the pool is
formed with radiated granite from Hiroshima.
Photo: Tadao Ando Architect and Associates*

Sunlight is cast across base of the pool, reflecting off the textured radiated granite bottom.
Photos: Tadao Ando Architect and Associates

View of the cylindrical concrete meditation space amid the UNESCO headquarters buildings.

Site plan

Site plan

A beam of sunlight moves into the space through the simple cut opening in the concrete wall.
Photo: Tadao Ando Architect and Associates

The simple cut opening in the formed-concrete wall links to the walkway beyond and casts light across the ground plane. A narrow slot of light from above subtly washes the wall as it falls.
Photo: Stephan Couturier

Retreats

The rapid pace and multiple demands of our daily lives requires that we seek balance in alternative modes of activity and relaxation. Designed for those who want to decompress during a frantic workweek or to take an extended break from the stress of the modern world, today's retreat environments cater to the individual mind and body. Whether focused around an abundance of natural healing waters, tucked deep within a sacred rain forest, or thoughtfully placed within a native ecosystem, retreat environments offer a temporary salve for what ails us. We have moved beyond the basic need for physical fitness, now requiring mind and body fitness. Unlike our daily rituals, the retreat encourages the release of one's body armor and the opening of the psyche to the moment, letting go of time and place.

...the retreat encourages the release of one's body armor and the opening of the psyche to the moment, letting go of time and place.

experience, provides an intense and intimate contact with the senses—sights, sounds, taste, touch, smells—to calm, soothe, and nourish the soul. The intention is to leave this environment feeling much better—mentally, physically, and spiritually—than when you arrived.

The retreat, as a connection to nature, is finding new meaning within contemporary culture. Whether one vacations at an eco-camp, treks into the mountains on a vision quest, contemplates a night sky hoping for shooting stars, or thoughtfully works in the garden, the craving is for that link to nature that enables one to temporarily shed the myopic thoughts and ways of our modern world. We want meaning in our lives and in the places that we inhabit. Retreating to nature in some form, to reconnect with its simple, tranquil, and reflective presence, alters the mind.

Contemporary spas provide a retreat environment designed for individual restoration and rejuvenation, enabling participants to reconnect with their biological rhythms. Ancient cultures regarded bathing as a pleasurable experience, an escape from their daily round of work. In addition to water, massage, ointments, exercise, wet and dry heat, and exposure to the sun were used. The ritual of bathing has been a popular custom among all classes in numerous cultures throughout time; people went to baths not simply to wash but also to relax, socialize, and exercise. The spa environment, designed for bodily perception and

The contemporary retreat environment is something to behold. The comprehensive experience, centered around the unquantifiable sensations of sustenance, tranquillity, and pleasure, offers a profound sense of well-being that lingers. We must continue to be aware of our necessary link to nature, her cycles and rhythms, and to create retreat environments that honor this relationship, offering potential for life-enhancing experience.

Noëlle Spa for Beauty and Wellness
Stamford, Connecticut
Photo: Daniel Aubrey

Tassajara Bath House
Zen Mountain Center
CARMEL VALLEY, CALIFORNIA

The Bath House is part of the Tassajara Zen Mountain Center, which sits on a rugged, wooded site outside Carmel Valley. The center functions primarily as a Buddhist monastery but opens to visitors during the summer. The organization has an integral vision of mental, physical, and spiritual health that is promoted through meditation and teaching, special attention to organic growing and food preparation, physical work, and cleansing the body in the natural hot springs and creek at Tassajara.

The purpose of the Bath House is to increase all aspects of health, daily by the monks and seasonally by summer visitors, within a safe and secure environment. It is a place to cleanse both body and spirit, to contemplate, relax, and commune with nature.

The building is sited to provide maximum sun exposure from the south and access to the nearby creek and hot springs. The simple, clear building forms and floor plan enable the user to experience a similar clarity of mind while engaged in the ritual of bathing. The rough-sawn, barnlike exterior siding and small sloped roofs reflect the concept of simplicity that harmonizes with the bathing ritual while giving human scale to the buildings. Interior finishes are more refined, using a color palette of soft, natural beiges, grays, and greens. The height of the interior partitions was held down below the sloped ceilings to expose the roof framing system and create a sense of openness and light.

An awareness of the healing aspects of multisensory experience is reflected throughout the project. Radiant tile floors provide warmth and luxury, especially in the winter months when temperatures are cooler, making it easy and inviting to immerse the body in water. Exposed wood roof framing members provide a wonderful smell in the buildings and a subtle connection to the natural environment. Large wooden sliding glass doors create an extension to the surrounding natural landscape and allow for maximum airflow in the hot summer months and protection from cold winds in the winter. A series of pools with varying temperatures enables one to submerge in water that feels comfortable to the touch. Seating alcoves throughout the site offer a variety of opportunities for gathering and interaction. Every aspect of the building avoids complexity, confusion, and distraction, resulting in an environment that encourages reflection, relaxation, and a connection to nature.

The entire building opens to the sun deck on the south through a series of wooden sliding doors that allow maximum airflow in the hot summer months and protection from the cold winter winds.
Photos: Helen Degenhardt

Detail of post at ground level

Small, sloped, roof forms give human scale to the buildings and highlight the entry.

The height of the interior partitions was held below the sloped ceilings to expose the roof-framing system and create a sense of openness and light. Photos, this page: Helen Degenhardt

View across the site of the men's and women's bath entries

A simple gravel path leads across the landscape to the altar and the entry of the Bath House.
Photo: Helen Degenhardt

A continuous deck on the south side of the Bath House offers a connected sequence of opportunities for gathering that include sunbathing, plunges, steam rooms, and creek pools.
Photo: Annie Phillips

Noëlle Spa for Beauty and Wellness

STAMFORD, CONNECTICUT

To create a nurturing environment, I design for all the senses, including the spiritual aspect of one's experience of the space. Everyone has the right to light, and air, and harmonious, life-enhancing environments. I believe that design is a healing art.

Clodagh, Clodagh Design International

The spa experience begins at the wisteria-wrapped entry pavilion, constructed of cedar beams and antique columns. A curved pathway flanked with large containers of flowers leads to the entry.

All photos: Daniel Aubrey

A 16,000-square-foot (1,486.5-square-meter), two-story postwar office building was transformed into a soothing oasis of carefully orchestrated spaces that nurture the individual mentally, physically, and spiritually. The Noëlle Spa was designed to create a refuge from the chaos and stress of modern life. The desire to offer destination-type spa treatments and traditional salon services while incorporating group fitness, meditation, and yoga classes for both men and women required a sensitive choreography of movement patterns and functional relationships.

The spa experience begins at the wisteria-wrapped entry pavilion, constructed of cedar beams and antique columns. A curved pathway flanked with large containers of flowers leads to the entry. Inside, the senses are engaged with the sound of chimes and running water, the fresh scent of essential oils, rich and varied surface textures, and a lush palette of color. The public areas are designed with massive, curved, hand-plastered walls embedded with straw and branded with images. The quieter, more private treatment rooms are defined with design elements that evoke a Zen-like serenity, such as translucent shoji-style glass panels, tatami mats, and views to a Japanese garden. Earth colors of ocher, terra cotta, and sage green are used throughout. Careful use of nontoxic materials and environmentally sound paints and finishes "is born of respect for people and for the world in which we live." The natural materials of concrete, glass, stainless steel, and bronze, and the Tuscan-influenced finishes on plaster walls "lend a sense of weight, permanence, and integrity to the spaces."[1]

[1]Clodagh

The Meditation Room is designed using traditional Japanese details and finishes such as appropriate shoe storage under the step, tatami mats, and shoji doors with rice paper.

A large skylight illuminates the atrium where artwork and spa products are displayed.

The spa corridor is troweled in rich colors of faded celadon, ocher, and amber plaster. Doors are washed to resemble eroded metal. The sconces and leaning pilasters function as doors to interior storage cabins in the treatment rooms, so laundry can be removed and replaced without disrupting the client.

A massive partial wall of khaki plaster and golden straw defines the atrium stair. Warm light from the skylight above washes over the wall, inviting people to the second floor.

The spa waiting area, defined by concrete columns and translucent over-head fabric structures, offers a comfortable and calming pre-treatment environment.

Custom cast-aluminum sinks hang between storage cabinets that efficiently disguise towel disposal in the men's spa area. Hand-worked, nontoxic plaster walls in a rich amber color frame this space.

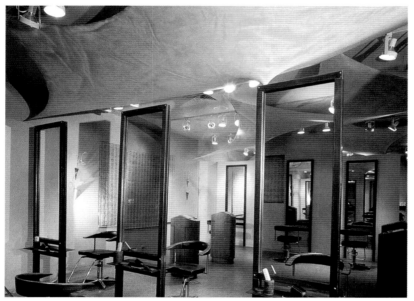

In the open styling room, simple cold-rolled steel-work stations are lined up in a rhythmic pattern. Comfortable chairs with built-in back support face mirrors accentuated by diffused light. A translucent fabric structure helps to define the ceiling plane and to diffuse light.

Lacquered Burmese trays and subtle shadowed lighting supplement the minimal environment of the wash area. The glowing tented ceiling ensures that clients are not dazzled by lights when lying back during the hair-washing process.

A cluster of cherrywood reception desks, routed and carved like primitive sculpture, are placed to give easy access to both staff and clients. The concrete floors are washed with color and the monolithic plaster walls guide one toward the spa areas.

Kohala Mountain Camps

NORTH KOHALA, HAWAII

Kohala Mountain Camps is designed as an environmentally friendly eco-camp consisting of 15 acres (6 hectares) of land situated within a larger parcel in the district of North Kohala, an area once used for growing and harvesting sugar cane. The camps project will provide economic benefits to the region by developing an important parcel of the land while preserving and enhancing it. The planning of Kohala Mountain Camps was influenced by the deeply spiritual views of nature held by the people of North Kohala. Five guiding principles form the basis for decisions on the project: respect for the land and the community, cultural preservation, education, health and wellness, and economic self-sustainability.

The facility will consist of one hundred vernacular tent-cottages equipped with bathroom facilities, bedding, and minimal furnishings, built on raised piers to minimize disturbance of the natural terrain. Guests will be able to experience living off the grids of electricity, water, and sewer, with each cottage relying on solar or wind power, a natural spring feed or catchment water system, and composting or low-flush toilets. An open-air pavilion includes dining facilities, classrooms, treatment rooms, and spa facilities with basic amenities. A variety of outdoor activities on land and at sea will provide the guest with intimate contact with the natural environment. Kohala Mountain Camps believes that it is healing and restorative to directly experience nature. Living lightly on the land and in harmony with nature will be a learning experience for guests, as well as an escape and retreat, helping to transform the consciousness of all involved: guests, staff, and the local community.

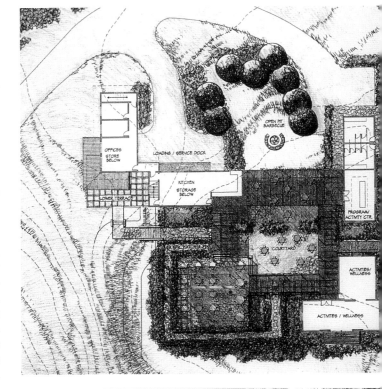

Top:
Plan of the central facilities, including dining area, classrooms, treatment rooms, and spa facilities with basic amenities.

Right:
Plan of tent layout with paths that link to the main circulation route.

All photos, plans, and drawings:
Wank Adams Slavin Associates

What remains of an existing taro field is considered historic.

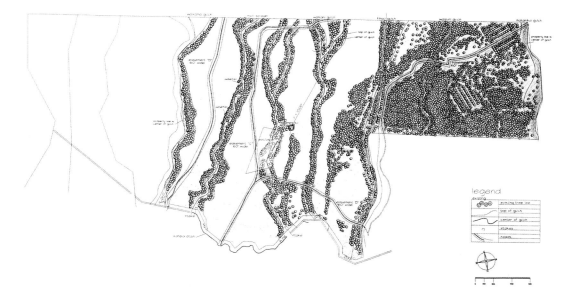

Existing site plan
Credits: Patricia Crow, ASLA

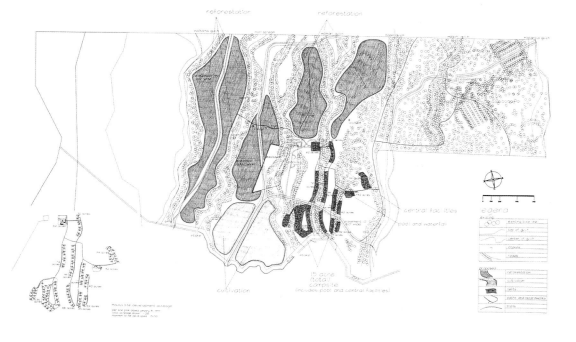

Land-use plan

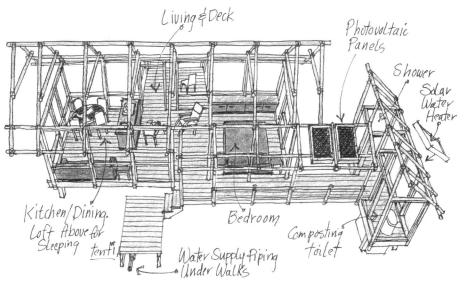

Living & Deck

Photovoltaic
Panels

Shower
Solar
Water
Heater

Kitchen/Dining.
Loft Above for
Sleeping

tent!

Bedroom

Composting
toilet

Water Supply Piping
Under Walks

Above:
An open plan/diagram of the tent-cottage and its simple amenities.

Left:
A waterfall speaks to the natural beauty of the site and the necessity of preserving it.

Carefully constructed walkways keep visitors safe and protect the natural environment from excess foot traffic.

J Hadley
96
Kohala walk

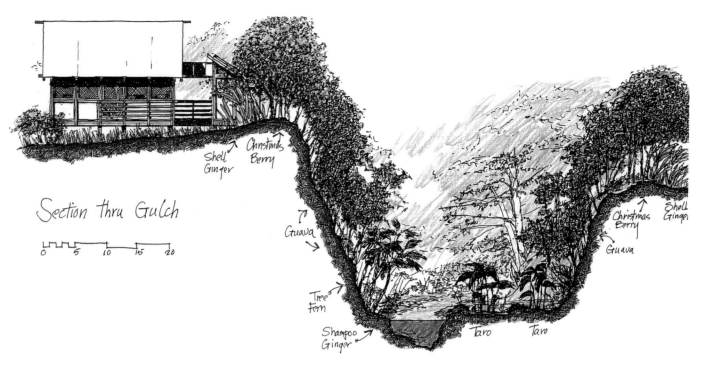

Section thru Gulch

0 5 10 15 20

Shell Ginger

Christmas Berry

Guava

Tree Fern

Shampoo Ginger

Taro Taro

Christmas Berry

Shell Ginger

Guava

Section through an existing gulch on the site with a tent-cottage above.

Tree Cover at Gulch

W.C.

Office

Open Pit Cooking Area

Kitchen

Offices

Store

Service/Loading Dock

Open Use: Yoga Treatment/Learning

View to Ocean

Hale

Kohala
Jim Kelley
'96

A bird's-eye view of the central facilities, including dining area,
classrooms, treatment rooms, and spa facilities with basic amenities.

Chopra Center for Well Being

LA JOLLA, CALIFORNIA

Dr. Deepak Chopra, a forerunner in mainstreaming the concept of the mind-body connection, has blended the Eastern wisdom and practice of Ayurveda with contemporary Western therapeutic modalities to create the Chopra Center for Well Being. Designed as a retreat from the everyday world experience, the center's purpose is to transport the client to an old-world environment to experience the therapeutic healing process. Dr. Chopra and his staff assembled from around the world an expert team of advisors in areas such as spa design, Eastern art and old-world artifacts, feng-shui, and earth-friendly finishes to ensure that the desired feeling was created in harmony with an environment that supported healing and well-being.

Housed in a renovated two-story building in downtown La Jolla, the center offers a small cafe and retail store, flexible classroom space, six treatment rooms, meditation and reading rooms, private conference areas, outdoor patios, staff amenities, and executive suites. An enormous amount of thought was given to the natural materials selected to enhance the sense of well-being within the environment, from textural finishes artistically hand-troweled on the walls to the unique fabrics, hand-crafted glass, and wood. Many transition areas have small insets of randomly placed handmade glass or tile that catch the light, adding another layer of richness and charm. On the ground level, the sound of a simple water feature bounces playfully off tile and plaster surfaces and greets guests as they pass into the treatment area. Every effort was taken to reinforce the connection to nature while providing a peaceful, nurturing, multisensory experience for both clients and staff.

Artisans from France used all-natural materials to create rich textural wall finishes and faux stone around the doorways, adding a rich layer of detail and contributing to the old-world feeling.

All photos: Glenn Cormier

The building facade is understated and blends nicely with downtown La Jolla. Community tours are offered to explain unknowns about the center. Patio dining, a small retail shop, and a variety of classes are open to the public daily.

Above:
The meditation room features three types of seating to accommodate the needs of all clients and an altar containing rare artifacts from India. The round window symbolizes nurturing and offers natural light to enhance the textures and color of the hand-troweled walls.

Right:
The cafe is designed to offer light, healthy fare to the visitor and opens to the outdoors, where patio dining can be enjoyed much of the year.

Facing page:
The design intent is to transport the visitor from everyday life into an old-world Eastern culture through the use of materials, finishes, color, and design details such as the domed ceiling, the intricately tiled archways, and the welcoming curved form of the reception counter.

The reading room offers a quiet, comfortable environment to be used between consultations. Warm colors and textures and overstuffed furniture provide a residential library setting where printed materials and videos about treatments can be viewed.

Treatment rooms are designed for efficiency while providing a calming environment for the client. Ambient lighting on the walls, combined with a small amount of daylight, provide balance and mood. Wood cabinetry and Eastern artifacts reinforce the old-world feeling.

Facing page:
The calming sound of water draws the guest down the hallway and into the treatment areas. The tiled archways and troweled textural walls add to the experiential quality of this healing environment.

Javana Spa

MOUNT SALAK, JAVA, INDONESIA

Javana Spa is located in a rain forest south of Jakarta on the cool slopes of Mount Salak. Literally, the earth breathes at this spot. The surrounding region is punctured with more than thirty active volcanoes that regularly erupt and replenish the tropical soils. The crater of Mt. Salak issues sulfurous mud and steam and has been recognized for centuries as a spiritual place for healing energy and renewal by the Sundanese. Local shamans, Surya Kencana, meditate in the caves behind the waterfalls of the mountainous crater because west Javanese people believe that all natural forces converge at this site.

The buildings of Javana Spa are perched like an eyrie on a level clearing surrounded by rain forest. The manicured grounds and Japanese-inspired gardens, imbued with a sense of order and rigidity, form an oasis and create an interface with the rich natural environment. The guest rooms open to private patio gardens with the forest edge of Mt. Salak only 109.5 yards (100 meters) away. Typical Javanese construction features a window wall with French doors and a continuous grated transom above for air circulation, inviting nature indoors day and night. Accommodations are minimal yet refined to ensure a quiet meditative experience without distraction. Public and private spaces spill out onto decks and garden environments for exercise classes and meditation. Water travels around all the buildings in narrow streams, waterfalls, and koi ponds, enabling quests to be in subtle yet constant contact with its calming sound.

Vegetables and herbs used for meals and treatments are grown on the premises and are chosen for their cleansing and healing properties. To enjoy the healing sulfurous waters, guests can hike the mountain or relax in the Oseng, the Japanese natural bath that collects the hot spring water brought directly to the spa from the volcano's caldera. The pristine rain forest offers a wide variety of sensory experiences that cycle throughout the day. Many animals and insects, as well as a wide range in weather conditions, create a wondrous symphony that engages all the senses.

The gardens that surround the gym and treatment areas include a waterfall and koi pond.

All photos: Smith Asbury, Inc.

Nestled into the slopes of Mt. Salak at an elevation of 3,937 feet (1,200 meters), Javana Spa is modeled after a Japanese honjin inn.

Filtered water is circulated over rocks from the crater that contain sulfur, adding minerals to the hot spring waters of the Onseng spa. From the spa, one can view the valley floor below.

Guest rooms open directly to a terrace and surrounding gardens, providing outdoor areas for quiet and solitude.

Entry to Javana Spa, located in the pristine rain forest on the slopes of Mt. Salak, 35.5 miles (54 kilometers) south of Jakarta.

The salon treatment areas have a wonderful sense of openness and light, and a strong relationship to the surrounding rain forest.

The exercise studio opens directly to the outdoors and is sited for maximum views and quality of natural light, thus reducing the need for artificial light.

The water garden, which can be viewed from the main lobby and the dining area, is one of the many formal gardens on the site.

The dining terrace, adjacent to the main dining room, offers a pleasant environment for morning meals.

Above:
As part of the surrounding garden, the Onseng hot spa provides a meditative retreat for guests.

Right:
Each guest room opens to a terrace, gardens, and the forest beyond, which offers a chorus of wondrous sound.

Above:
Guests contemplate the view to
the valley floor below.

Left:
The pond draws a variety of native
birds to the site.

Institutional / Educational Spaces

*H*istorically, the perception of public institutions and their buildings has been one of power and monumentality; they embody a community's commitment to constructing buildings that reflect this ideal. The individual was not recognized in this environment, a system perceived as much larger and much greater than the needs of human beings. Over time, social and financial implications altered the character of these spaces. Thought shifted to the pragmatics of constructing institutional settings, resulting in spaces that were restricted, demoralizing, devoid of character, and lacking the ability to creatively engage the immediate or surrounding community and environment.

Trends today are offering signs that the individual is being heard and honored. There has been a subtle shift from the concept of serving a system to the serving of the individual. There is a recognition that a link does exist between that which is created and constructed and the neighborhood and environment that surrounds it, as well as the people who inhabit it. In many ways, some contemporary institutional settings are being viewed as small communities or villages within a larger context, enabling them to more specifically address the needs of citizenry. How spaces are created within that community to nurture and sustain well-being, and to promote individual empowerment, is seen in the ultimate human success of the

There has been a subtle shift from the concept of serving a system to the serving of the individual.

facility. From the public school where the notion of the talking head is becoming passé to the mental-health center that embraces the individual in a homelike setting, there is an awareness of the correlation between environment and use. Does the environment reflect the participant in scale and architectural form? Does it respond to culture by age group, discipline, ethnicity, or by another model, and offer specific identity? Does it create a safe environment while providing the opportunity to explore and learn?

Institutions today are in a rapid state of change, and the individuals who inhabit their realms have the potential to define and improve their meaning and influence for subsequent generations. Consequently, an institutional arena can no longer be considered a static container for service and learning but a place where one is actively engaged through interaction with the environment. An understanding that the institution is reflected in how the day-to-day environment is transformed by its participants creates an opportunity to facilitate wonder and to empower the participants within that environment. The intention is that these empowered individuals, the products of learning, working, and interacting within a fully participatory environment, will point the way for the successful evolution and integration of their communities and its institutions.

Center for AIDS Services
Oakland, California
Photo: David Wakely

Ventana Vista Elementary School

T U C S O N ,   A R I Z O N A

Lying at the base of Tucson's Santa Catalina mountains, Ventana Vista Elementary School is unlike most traditionally planned schools. Responding to its Sonoran desert locale and topography, a rich learning environment is created through the use of forms, texture, pattern, color, and degrees of light and shadow. Based on a series of courtyards and passages pinwheeling around a centralized two-story library, the school itself is a teaching tool.

Thought of as a city for children, the school is organized as a group of different "neighborhoods," with the communal desert kaleidoscope inhabiting the space between the library and the multipurpose area. Each neighborhood takes on its own distinct architectural characteristics that become easily identifiable and homelike to the students. The courtyards that correspond to each neighborhood are scaled to that age group, providing seating and areas for teaching, experimentation, and discovery. The kindergarten and first-grade court is smaller and more compressed, with at-grade windows and spy holes. The second and third graders are recipients of a solstice wall, which tracks the sun and honors the calendar. The fourth- and fifth-grade court features a chalkboard graffiti wall and encourages individual expression. Consequently, as children advance from grade to grade, their growing bodies are reflected in the scale and forms of the architecture and their school identity shifts to a new neighborhood icon. The building as a whole creates a unique educational environment that nurtures children in familiar neighborhood settings, fostering the process of discovery campuswide while encouraging exploration of the surrounding desert ecosystem.

Top:
Courtyards correspond to "neighborhoods"
that are scaled to each age group, providing
seating and areas for teaching, experimenta-
tion, and discovery.

Left:
Responding to its Sonoran desert locale and
topography, this earth-bound city for children
offers a rich learning environment created
through the use of forms, texture, pattern,
color, and degrees of light and shadow.

All photos: Timothy Hursley
All plans and drawings: Antoine Predock Architect

Shaded by a geometric metal screen, the solstice terrace offers the desert light experience of pattern and shadow.

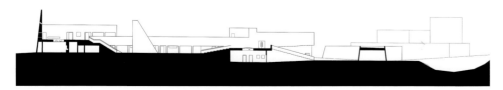

Section through third- and fourth-grade neighborhoods, desert kaleidoscope

Unlike most traditionally planned schools, the total environment is a teaching tool. The entry of the school, protected from the desert elements, is tucked to the right of the tilted landscape wall.

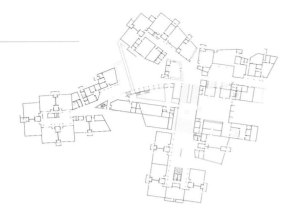

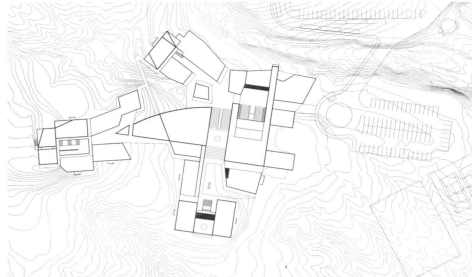

Floor plan, level one

Site plan

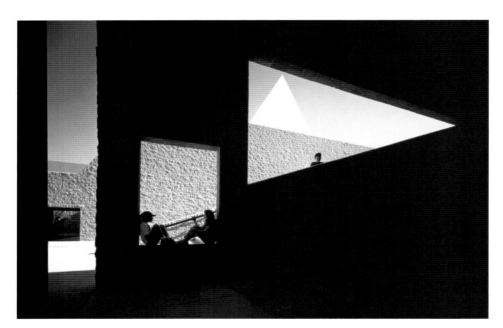

Left:
A block wall at the entry to the library, with openings for seating and views, frames the central staircase from the B-52 courtyard. The nomadic tent structure that covers the multi-purpose room is seen beyond.

Below:
The graffiti wall that is part of the fourth- and fifth-grade courtyard provides an evolving palette for individual expression and creativity.

The carefully modulated apertures of the solstice wall are designed to spotlight story disks on significant days of the year. The wall provides a continuous source of thought and exploration for students and teachers.

Center for AIDS Services

OAKLAND, CALIFORNIA

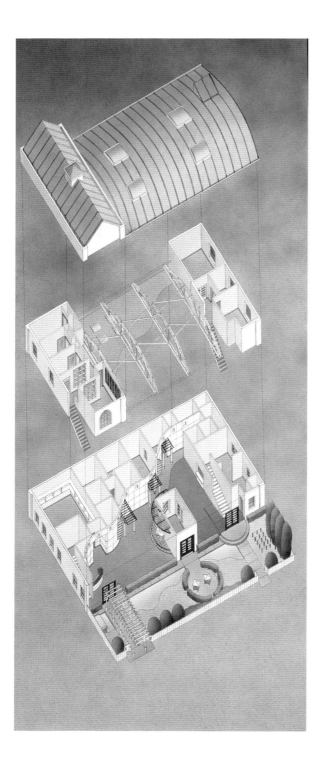

The Center for AIDS Services is a 6,200-square-foot (576-square-meter) day-use facility for people living with AIDS/HIV in Oakland, California. The existing loft building had been a grocery store, a church, and, most recently, offices. The design team's charge was to create a sense of hope and community in an industrial space.

The existing facility was approximately 80 percent gutted, with several walls and two mezzanines being incorporated into the design as a cost-saving measure. Ceilings were left exposed in public areas to take advantage of existing skylights that infuse the space with natural light. At the heart of the design is the integration of the functional components of the center, encouraging interaction between staff and clients. However, it was critical to divide the space into public and private function areas. A serpentine wall inserted diagonally across the space achieves this goal. On one side, existing partitions and low ceilings with borrowed light from above define more private functions such as food bank, massage, and counseling. On the other side, a large, open, full-height public space houses the living and dining rooms. "What is most wonderful about the design is the curving wall," says the center's executive director, Jerry De Jong. "It almost acts as an arm that reaches out and encircles people." Corner windows subtly jutting out from the wall address the need for security by providing opportunity for observation and supervision. The administrative offices of the center are located on the mezzanines.

AIDS does not distinguish between color, religion, race, sex, age, or social status; consequently, people from all walks of life find themselves at the center sharing space and activities. Residential elements such as the fireplace, piano, and a television room are areas where clients find comfort and familiarity and tend to gather. A soft color palette of teal, pewter, and plum, complemented with indirect and natural lighting, provides a calming atmosphere for clients and staff. Completed entirely through gifts, the Center for AIDS Services reflects community outreach and heartfelt support.

Left:
Exploded axonometric rendering

Facing page:
Ceilings were left exposed in public areas to take advantage of skylights that infuse the space with natural light. The sculptural serpentine wall separates public and private functions and offers niches for art and playful openings for borrowed light.

All photos: David Wakely
All site plans: Elbasani & Logan Architects

Ground-floor plan

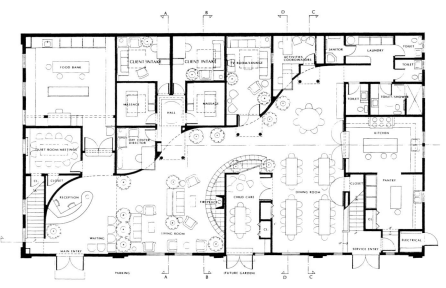

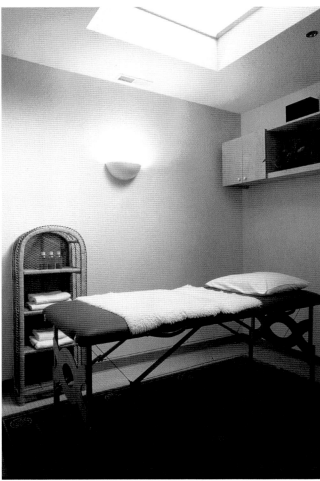

One of the center's essential services is therapeutic massage, offering the healing power of touch to people living with AIDS/HIV.

The center offers both group activities and quiet places where one can meditate and reflect in solitude. An area of the wall is recessed to create a small altar space.

Facing page:
Corner windows that jut out from the serpentine wall address the need for security through observation and supervision. Residential elements such as the fireplace and the piano offer comfort and familiarity to the client.

The television room has proven to be a favorite gathering spot for the center's clients. Its residential feeling promotes comfort and easy use.

A serpentine wall inserted diagonally across the space divides it into public and private function areas. The fireplace is the heart of the living room, lending a residential feel to the facility.

People from all walks of life find themselves sharing meals together in the dining room. A child-care center divides the main living areas from the dining area.

Sinte Gleska University

ANTELOPE, SOUTH DAKOTA

This landscape and its people have had a healing effect on us as well, and continue to remind us of the balance necessary to a healthy existence.

RoTo Architects, Inc.

The planning, siting, and design of the new campus for Sinte Gleska University, the first and oldest tribal university in the Americas, is a collaborative exploration seeking contemporary forms to express traditional values and practices. The process is inspired by the spatial and diagrammatic structure of the traditional Lakota systems of movement and rest, the formal characteristics of the Lakota universal model, and Lakota numerology. This knowledge, recorded in the memory of elders, is expressed through stories, daily rituals, ceremonial dances, shelter constructions, and temporary settlements. For the Lakota, all things are interconnected and interdependent. At all sizes and scales the physical, aesthetic, and spiritual aspects are woven together.

Primary siting decisions and diagrams of the campus were based on a hierarchical system of connections that occur in reading the natural landscape through the Lakota lens. The campus plan attempts to integrate the man-made and the natural site conditions using spatial ordering systems defined as natural (experientially based), abstract (intellectually based), and mythological (spiritually based). Each campus building project is developed as an instrument for teaching vocational educational students the process, techniques, and skills of construction. Their design, construction logic, and building materials emerge from the belief that every aesthetic issue must be simultaneously practical. The Hexagon Building and the Technology Building were the first two buildings to be developed on the site using straw bales, tribally milled rough-sawn timbers, modular building components salvaged from a defunct military defense plant, and recycled concrete masonry units. "Our design process, which occurs on site [a member of RoTo has lived on the reservation since 1995] and in L.A., includes all media for visualizing and study. We draw. We model in paper and in wood. We model on the computer. All are necessary."[1] The project is a collaborative effort that will continue to evolve for some years.

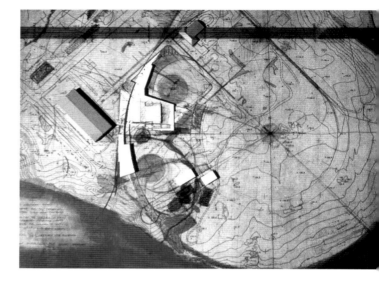

The ruin of the main path that children walked on for many years to a missionary boarding school led to a point that became a clear center for an earth-based observatory. An early site model demonstrates how the location and massing of the architecture could respond to the Lakota star knowledge.

[1]RoTo Architects, Inc.
All plans and drawings: RoTo Architects, Inc.

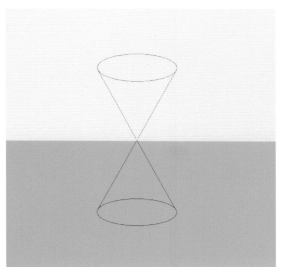

The Technology Building will house a new natural, physical, and computer-science curriculum funded by the National Science Foundation. The building (under construction) combines conventional and off-the-shelf technology with traditional and sustainable technologies. It is sited to frame the winter solstice sunrise and sunset.
Photo: RoTo Architects, Inc.

The roof structure of the Multipurpose Building is defined by the seven Lakota directions: up (sky), down (earth), north, south, east, west, and center (the point of convergence, the horizon). The relationship between earth and sky, a double vortex form called kapemni, is the symbol of the Lakota universe.
Photo: Benny Chan-Fotoworks

The site for the new campus of Sinte Gleska University was revealed by reading the natural landscape through the Lakota lens. It was learned that any existing condition could be transformed from negative to positive if it supported the telling of the stories of the Lakota people.
Photos: RoTo Architects, Inc.

The wacipi, *or powwow, is spiritual preparation combined with the physical stress and sacrifice of ritual dance to create the conditions for a human to become a conduit between earth and sky. For the Lakota, this connection must be maintained or the universe will perish.*

Constructed by faculty, staff, and students, the Student Center on the original campus of Sinte Gleska University was undertaken to test strategies and techniques to be used on the new site. Future straw-bale structures were modified based on knowledge gained from this construction.

The campus design strategy and heavy-timber framing of the east building of the Technology Complex provided enough potential orders for the tribal sawmill to enable the tribal government to upgrade equipment and employment at the mill.

Timber framing of the Technology Building demonstrates how the preengineered metal skin was cut to frame different exterior spaces and horizon events, such as the seven buttes on the south horizon, which have a Lakota story of their own.
Photos: RoTo Architects, Inc.

The north elevation of the Technology Building demonstrates the strategy of employing this type of structure to accommodate budget and time restrictions and shows how the simple forms of the local building type can be configured to support the telling of traditional Lakota myths and the teaching of traditional knowledge.

In addition to straw bales, construction materials for the Student Center building included tribally milled rough-sawn timbers, modular building components salvaged from a defunct military defense plant, and the ruin of a concrete masonry unit structure. The transformation of that ruin healed a long-standing wound for the university and helped to establish the trust of the community.

A ceremonial prairie fire was performed by the elders to purify and heal the land that was to become the new campus. The landscape and its people have had a healing affect on the design team; they serve as a reminder of the balance necessary to a healthy existence.

Health / Medical Spaces

Cultural values and societal trends have shaped our systems of healing throughout time, determining the design and objectives of the place where medicine is administered. The concept of medicine has evolved through multiple forms and meanings, forever striving to find balance between art and reality. From halls for dreamers in ancient times to the scientific curing machine of the modern era, the medical environment has seen many faces. As the cost of health care continues to rise, resulting in the drive to ration care and reduce costs, we have moved further toward the practical side of the scale and its implications.

Western medicine once had its foundation in the premise that a strong connection existed between mind and body. Regarding the patient as a member of a family, a community, a culture, and understanding those relationships, enabled healing to manifest. The technological advances of modern medicine led to the discovery of specific causes of and treatments for disease, which could be universally applied with great success. In turn, mind-body interactions and the complex needs of the individual patient were deemphasized and the medical environment became one of sterility, isolation, and fear. However, as our world continues to grow smaller, with fewer boundaries, a shared desire to explore the concept of healing in its broadest sense is emerging and a new medical paradigm is taking shape. Medicine is rediscovering the connection between mind and body and is being stretched to encompass what we value in society and who we are as human beings. Advances in

Medicine is rediscovering the connection between mind and body and is being stretched to encompass what we value in society and who we are as human beings.

technology have transformed the health-care environment in significant ways and there is great potential to continue that transformation as a result of honoring the mind-body connection.

Our global culture is fast becoming conscious of and dedicated to facets of our overall health and wellness—mental, physical, emotional, and spiritual. Our built environments are no exception. It has become increasingly evident that environments influence our behavior and shape our actions, thoughts, and emotions. As this new awareness begins to find its way into doctor's offices, clinics, and hospitals, the potential for healing and transformation for all who inhabit these spaces increases. In many respects, the territory offers a clean palette and will test the capacity to creatively push beyond the boundaries that currently frame health-care facility design. There are no formulas. There are historical precedents and their evidence can be observed in the gradual incorporation of such attributes as views to nature, homelike qualities, natural light, sacred geometries, and medicinal gardens. The design professions are being challenged to ensure that the environments they create contribute to the healing process. As the medical community considers the patient holistically, the designer must engage the environment in which that encounter occurs with a similar intent. Health care has come full circle in many respects. We continue to move forward with the technological care of disease and dying, and look to our past and culturally diverse roots as we strive to consider souls as well as bodies.

Facing page:
Good Samaritan Regional Medical Center, Healing Garden, Phoenix, Arizona
Photo: Michael Paulson

Therapeutic Garden for Children
Institute for Child and Adolescent Development
WELLESLEY, MASSACHUSETTS

The topographic model illustrates the new ridge-ravine carved by the rill.
Model: Douglas P. Reed, ASLA

On a 1-acre (.4-hectare) site adjacent to the Institute for Child and Adolescent Development, a therapeutic garden is an integral component of the treatment of behavioral disorders in traumatized children. It was developed as an environment where children and therapists could engage in treatment through the experience of a series of unprogrammed and evocative spaces, in addition to opportunities for play. The garden expresses the belief that interaction with landscape, designed for therapeutic purposes, enables a child to enter the deepest reaches of self.

The design expresses the narrative of a watercourse that weaves its way through the site, linking a sequence of spaces that correspond to stages of a child's recovery. The topography of the site was reshaped into a series of archetypal land forms carved by water: a cavelike ravine for safety and security, an upland wooded plateau for exploration, a mount for climbing, an island for seclusion, a pond for discovery, steep and shallow slopes that invite risk, and a large open glade for running and playing. The watercourse originates in a low granite basin on a terrace off the clinic playroom. Water bubbles up, spills over the basin's edge, and travels underground to emerge in a fieldstone seat wall. It then splashes into a steel-sided rill 8 inches (20 centimeters) wide that meanders through the garden and flows into a pond.

Masses of native plants frame the interior spaces of the garden and define areas of distinct character. The planting creates a seemingly random pattern of intimate places and expansive areas while modulating light and shade throughout the garden. By carefully layering the planting and land forms, the garden is never disclosed entirely from one vantage, encouraging the child to move through and discover the sequence of spaces.

The mount, when mowed, reveals the contours of its archetypal land form.

All photos: Douglas P. Reed, ASLA

The watercourse is the unifying element of the project and originates in a green granite basin on the terrace off the clinic playroom. Water spills over the rim of the basin, flows under the terrace, and emerges in a shallow basin.

The archetypal land form carved by the water, the mount is sometimes left unmowed to allow children to experience it as a meadow. The clinic is seen beyond.

The steel-sided rill weaves through the archetypal land form known as the ravine, a place of safety and security for the child.

The terrace extends directly off the clinic playroom and integrates lawn into its paving design.

The mount for climbing, left unmowed, creates a meadow environment for the children to experience and opens to a sun-filled glade beyond.

The rill winds its way through the landscape from a source near the clinic play terrace.

A view from the garden path looks out to the archetypal land forms that correspond to the stages of a child's recovery.

Water spills over the rim of a low granite basin on the play terrace, flows underground, emerges from stainless-steel pipes in the fieldstone seat wall, and spills into a shallow basin.

Hospital Santa Engracia

MONTERREY, NUEVO LEON, MEXICO

Set in the high-plain desert of Mexico, Hospital Santa Engracia accommodates a 4-acre (1.5-hectare) sloped site in a rapid-growth suburb of Monterrey. Designed as a full-service medical center, including a medical office building and multilevel parking garage, this state-of-the-art facility is the first hospital in the area built to United States standards. In its expressive and colorful architecture Santa Engracia reflects the cultural and economic issues that shape hospital design in Mexico today.

The irregular shape of the sloped land offered a unique opportunity to provide different levels of access for patients, staff, and physicians. Throughout the hospital, public and staff are separated as much as possible in an effort to minimize the anxiety that surrounds the medical environment. The ground-floor orientation is inward, configured in a quarter-circle that allows for spectacular views of the nearby mountains. Patient rooms are arranged in a cluster of four- and six-bed suites in the same quarter-circle layout. The cluster grouping allows access to rooms from a staff corridor rather than from the main circulation corridor, giving patients more privacy. The suites are spacious and reflect the importance given to family participation in providing comfort and care to the patient. Views to nature and the surrounding mountain range were key elements in creating an environment of health and healing. The reception area opens to lush gardens and the soothing sound of water, and all patient rooms have terraces with mountain views. Exterior circulation is clearly defined and offers the pleasant experience of vine-covered trellises, encouraging patients and staff to spend more time outside.

An entry courtyard fountain greets the visitor with the calming sound of water and garden views.

All photos: Mark Trew
All plans and drawings: Henningson, Durham & Richardson, Inc.

Terraces off patient rooms provide visiting areas for larger family gatherings. In addition, patients can enjoy the outdoors and magnificent mountain views.

Set in the high desert of Mexico, Santa Engracia's orientation on the site takes advantage of the dramatic mountain views. Natural scenery improves patients' attitudes, reminding them of the outside world, and minimizes the institutional feelings associated with medical environments by both patients and staff.

The exterior sculpted wall of the family waiting area expresses rich color and form as it moves people along an exterior walkway with distant mountain views.

Trellises provide shade and protection from the intense heat of the sun, allowing patients and staff to spend more time outside.

Conscious attention to lighting and color choice makes the labor and delivery room a soothing environment. To honor Mexican tradition, delivery rooms were designed to accommodate family members.

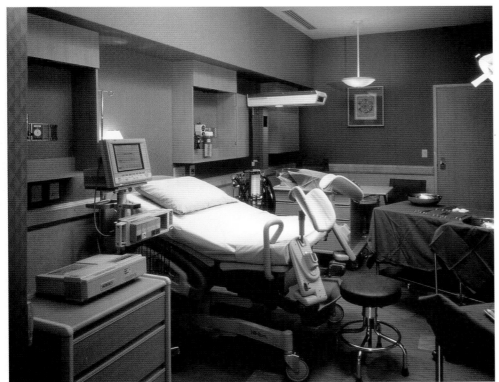

Floor plan, level one

Floor plan, level two

Health and Healing Clinic
Institute for Health and Healing
California Pacific Medical Center

SAN FRANCISCO, CALIFORNIA

The design for the Health and Healing Clinic was inspired by the joining of Eeastern and Western medicine and the institute's desire to create an environment that honors the body, mind, and spirit and sets the stage for the healing process to begin. The programs and services provided by the clinic integrate the knowledge and practice of contemporary medicine with appropriate complementary and alternative care. The 1,000-square-foot (93-square-meter) renovation of an existing medical suite includes a reception and sitting room and six exam and treatment rooms.

The furnishings, colors, light, and materials were all chosen to provide a positive experience for all the senses. The soothing sound of water greets visitors from a quiet fountain on the reception desk. A wooden screen behind the fountain blocks a view of the computer as you enter. Potted bamboo creates a natural protective barrier for guests and brings nature into the space. Comfortable wooden chairs covered with a violet chenille fabric provide a feeling of warmth in the sitting area. Violet is the color of the brow chakra and is associated with the qualities of higher consciousness and wisdom. A round upholstered ottoman serves as a footrest or as additional seating when needed. The antique Japanese tansu behind the reception desk serves as storage for office supplies. It also expresses a sense of history, with its roots in the ancient eastern cultures from which many of the clinic's complementary therapies originate.

The exam rooms have a home-like feeling, with wooden dressers for storage, indirect light from table lamps and upholstered rattan patient chairs. A mirror above the dresser honors a patient's need to "recompose" themselves in private after their exam or treatment is complete. Flower vases are hung on the walls in the hallway to bring life into this narrow space and to provide a seasonal display that reflects the cycles of life.

Art makes an important contribution to the care of the soul. The labyrinth image is used as a symbol and a metaphor for the inner healing journey in several works of art featured in the space. This painting, by Juliet Wood, serves as an intuitive and meditative aid that can draw one's focus inward.

All photos: David Livingston

The clinic's design was inspired by the joining of Eastern and Western medicine. The warmth of the wooden tansu cabinets greets guests as they enter. Potted bamboo brings nature indoors and helps to soften the corners of the sitting area.

Wood is used for the cabinets in the doctors charting area, adding warmth to the space and a visual link to the waiting area where the same wood is used for the tansu. The chair provides additional seating for patients who may need to be present during this phase of their visit.

A fountain at the clinic entrance brings the sound of nature indoors and creates a soothing atmosphere for visitors as well as staff. The antique Japanese screen behind the fountain provides an attractive visual barrier between the computer and the visitors as they enter the clinic.

To create a non-institutional environment, wooden dressers are used for storage in the exam rooms and table lamps provide soft, indirect lighting. A mirror is provided so patients can "recompose" themselves in private, after a treatment.

Joel Schnaper Memorial Garden
Terence Cardinal Cooke Health Center

NEW YORK, NEW YORK

Located in east Harlem across from Central Park, the Terence Cardinal Cooke Health Center's AIDS unit is home for 156 residents infected with HIV. An adjacent 3,000-square-foot (278.5-square-meter) sensory rooftop garden provides a therapeutic outdoor environment for the unit, a key component of their day-to-day therapy.

Nowhere do gardens offer a more poignant response to the sense of individual crisis in illness than in the challenges of HIV/AIDS. Through the opportunistic infections and complex symptoms of HIV-associated illness, abilities vary daily, magnifying feelings of vulnerability and isolation. Most patients are so ill that a quick fix, like caressing a rosemary bush or running fingers through water, is what is needed. As illness limits personal choices, the garden enriches those choices. It addresses changing physical and emotional needs by offering opportunity and a rich sensory experience, whatever the individual's capacity.

The design focuses on the specific needs and requirements of the HIV-infected resident. Numerous concerns are addressed, including strength and stamina, varying sensory abilities, sunlight sensitivity, awareness, orientation and the need for activity, interaction, privacy, and independence. Immediate and constant sensory stimulation, especially of sound and scent, became a common denominator for many patient needs. Wind chimes with varying tonal qualities were strategically placed throughout the garden, and the fragrance of plants, herbs, and flowers give sensory clues to the user. Texture was important, both in constructed surfaces and plant materials. Plants that attract butterflies and a kinetic wind sculpture can be seen from patient rooms, offering visual interest for patients not well enough to venture outside. Accessible planters used for horticultural therapy connect the garden to the center's physical and occupational therapy programs, advancing the therapeutic value of nature as a complement to conventional medical and social programs.

The design for the Joel Schnaper Memorial Garden responds to the human heart and stimulates the senses, creating a life-enhancing experience for all who visit. It illustrates the powerful connection of nature, healing, and palliative care. The garden demonstrates that therapy-focused outdoor environments can provide a direct and humane response to the demand on increasingly limited resources and broaden our understanding of providing compassionate care. The garden is dedicated to a landscape architect who died of AIDS.

A tilted watering can pours water into a plant-filled trough. Using a concealed recirculating pump, this inexpensive fountain provides a pleasant buffer to the surrounding city noise as well as a delightful opportunity to place a hand under pouring water.
Photo: David Kamp

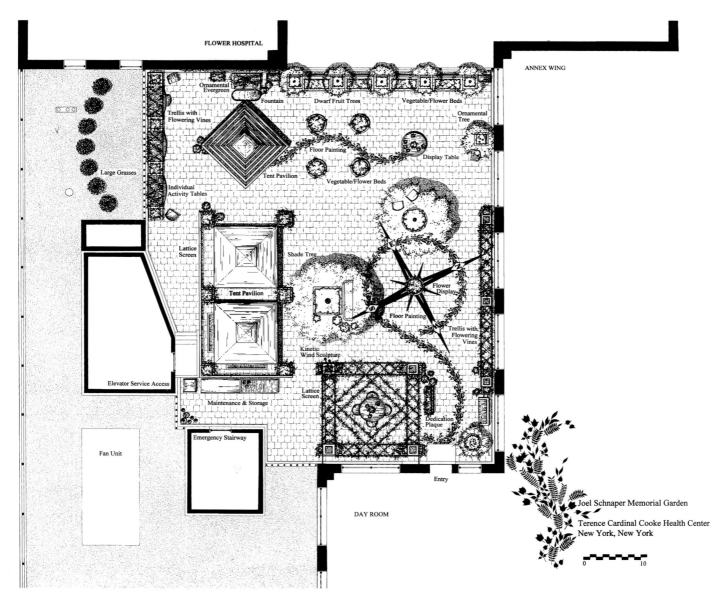

FLOWER HOSPITAL

ANNEX WING

Ornamental Evergreen

Fountain

Dwarf Fruit Trees

Vegetable/Flower Beds

Ornamental Tree

Trellis with Flowering Vines

Floor Painting

Display Table

Large Grasses

Tent Pavilion

Vegetable/Flower Beds

Individual Activity Tables

Lattice Screen

Shade Tree

Tent Pavilion

Flower Display

Floor Painting

Trellis with Flowering Vines

Kinetic Wind Sculpture

Elevator Service Access

Maintenance & Storage

Lattice Screen

Dedication Plaque

Emergency Stairway

Fan Unit

Entry

DAY ROOM

Joel Schnaper Memorial Garden

Terence Cardinal Cooke Health Center
New York, New York

0   10

Site plan
Plan: Dirtworks

Top:
The garden is fully accessible, enabling individuals to experience it without assistance. Vine-covered lattice columns and trellises adjacent to resident windows frame views, provide shade, and display horticultural therapy projects for residents confined indoors.
Photo: John M. Hall

Above:
The planters vary in size and height for individual ease of use. Central planters are circular, providing an easily accessible demonstration area for displays, group activities, and planting instruction.
Photo: David Kamp

Top:
The garden offers a choice of protective settings, from open sky to dappled shade under trellises and trees to complete shade under tent structures. These spaces are flexible in size and arrangement to accommodate large events as well as private, quiet moments.
Photo: John M. Hall

Above:
Stenciled floor paintings of leaves from plants used in the garden provide interest and orientation. A graceful path flows from the lounge area and encircles a compass and flower display. Other areas have distinctive "rugs," providing amusement for visiting children.
Photo: David Kamp

Yacktman Children's Pavilion
Lutheran General Hospital
PARK RIDGE, ILLINOIS

The entry pavilion is a three-story atrium wrapped in vividly colored and boldly patterned mosaic tile. The sky-lit ceiling features a spiral constellation of lights. Children love to yell and laugh in this space, hearing their voices echo of the tile.
Photos: A. Semborian/Cesar Pelli & Associates

Lutheran General Hospital has a wide variety of primary care and multispecialty practices scattered around its campus in a complicated network of sites. The goal for the Yacktman Children's Pavilion was to provide one highly identifiable location for all outpatient pediatric clinics as well as children's ambulatory diagnostic and treatment services. The 88,000-square-foot (8,175-square-meter) Children's Pavilion balances innovation and practicality with the intention of creating a nurturing environment for children and their families.

The forms of the building are animated by light and color. Tones of green, orange, gold, and yellow are rooted in the autumnal landscape of the Midwest. A spiraling cylinder marks the pavilion entry, clad in ocher-colored stone and punctured by a grid of square openings. Echoing the main hospital campus, the west facade is a decorative pattern of warm-colored brick. A critical aspect of the pavilion design was to reduce the fear and confusion common in medical settings and offer a welcoming and cheerful experience for the families who visit. A curving stair and balconies provide changing views from inside the drum-shaped three-story atrium, wrapped in vividly colored mosaic tile. The many square openings filter natural light that softly changes as the sun moves across the sky. The sky-lit ceiling features a spiral constellation of lights in a space that lifts the spirits.

A choreographed sequence of spatial experiences invites people on a journey that unfolds over time. A unique way-finding system establishes a distinct theme for each level: under-the-sea, astronomy, and a rain forest. To contain costs, the colorful graphics were implemented by the hospital's engineering staff using templates developed by the design team. Each exam room has a custom designed seating area and workstation that responds to family-centered care and encourages interaction between the physician, patient, and family members.

Designed to be friendly, cheerful, and welcoming, the Yacktman Children's Pavilion features a cylindrical drum clad in an ocher-hued Minnesota stone and punctured by a grid of square openings, and a playful entrance canopy.

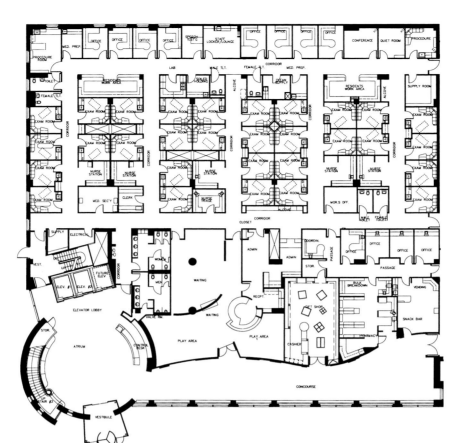

Entry-level floor plan
Plan: Watkins Carter Hamilton
Architects, Inc., in association with
Cesar Pelli & Associates

A day-lit concourse, with an abstract cityscape theme, links the lobby, gift
shop, pharmacy, coffee shop, and patient-relations office to the atrium.
Photos, above and facing: Jud Haggard Photography

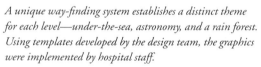

*A unique way-finding system establishes a distinct theme
for each level—under-the-sea, astronomy, and a rain forest.
Using templates developed by the design team, the graphics
were implemented by hospital staff.*

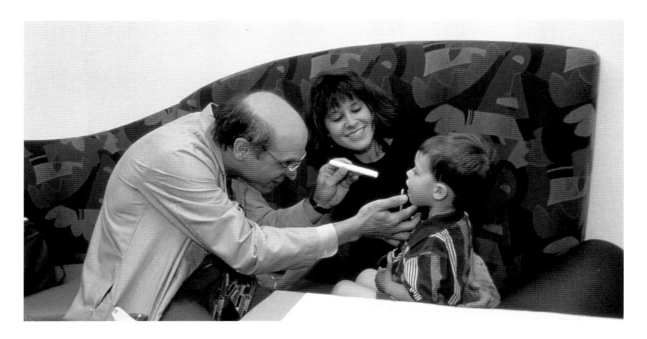

*Each exam room has a custom-designed seating area and workstation to
accommodate family-centered care and to encourage interaction among the
physician, patient, and family.*
Photos: Jud Haggard Photography

The waiting rooms were designed to have enough floor space to play with toys, while fish tanks provide a positive distraction. The way-finding theme continues with the use of colorful wall friezes.

Beausejor Retirement Home

AUNAY-SUR-ODON, FRANCE

Located in a small town in the Normandy region of France, the Beausejor Retirement Home is a long-stay residence patterned after a small village. The 45,000-square-foot (4,180.5-square-meter) facility is composed of four buildings and is part of a larger hospital complex, yet functions independently, except for ancillary services. The program called for a facility with a humble background, a place that encourages communication, promotes social life, and enhances joy for each resident.

Designed as a village set around a central garden, the buildings are modulated in clusters that accommodate six individuals. Resembling the scale of a single-family house, each cluster contains a living room and kitchen in addition to private and semiprivate bedrooms. The absence of corridors offers the resident the ability to move through a series of linked spaces without the monotony of following one continuous path; way-finding is eased by a memorable theme associated with each floor. At each level, large wood-floored terraces greet the sun. The buildings are situated to provide a variety of views to the central garden. This village square offers a multitude of sensory experiences and activities including water features, pathways, wood benches, a variety of plant life, a winter garden, craft shops, and a restaurant. An aviary provides a constant and lively show for the residents, a source of conversation, and the activity and joy of feeding the birds. Architectural materials blend stone, wood, metal, and glass for a contemporary image. Interior furnishings and finishes reflect a balance of past and present, offering a sense of familiarity and home to the residents. According to the owner, the project improved the quality of health care through enhanced staff performance, increased visitor and community participation, and higher resident satisfaction ratings.

The village square offers a multitude of sensory experiences and activities including water features, pathways, wood benches, a variety of plant life, a winter garden, craft shops, a restaurant, and an aviary.

All photos: Michael Moch

Designed as a long-stay residence for 100 people, this retirement facility is patterned after a small village and is built around a central garden, the village square.

The aviary is a constant and lively show for the residents, providing a source of conversation and the activity and joy of feeding the birds.

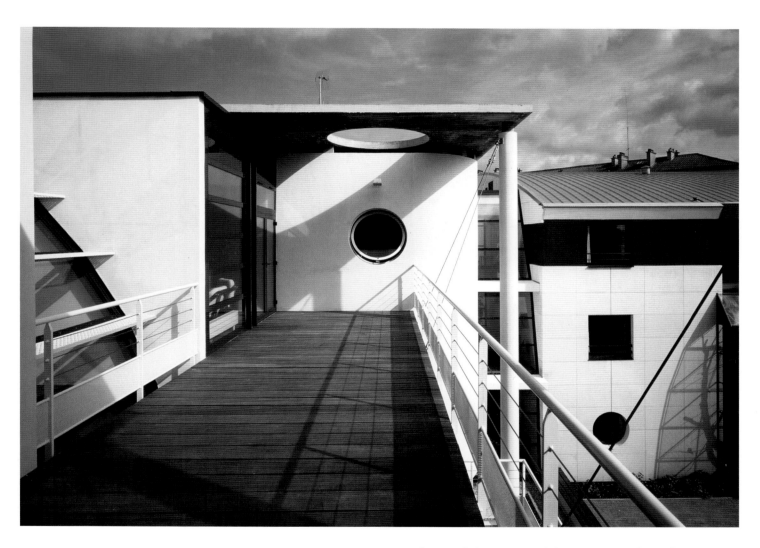

The sunny deck terraces on each floor encourage residents to be outside. End walls that separate the interior and exterior diminish the anxiety of retreating back indoors.

Healing Garden
Good Samaritan Regional Medical Center
PHOENIX, ARIZONA

Good Samaritan Regional Medical Center is a high-rise presence in downtown Phoenix. At the heart of the campus is a 15,000-square-foot (1393.5-square-meter) overstructure courtyard that has been transformed into a healing garden. Designed as a place of relaxation, reflection, and renewal for the entire hospital community—patients and their families, employees, physicians, volunteers, and visitors—Good Samaritan's Healing Garden is unique within a health-care setting.

The creation of multisensory experience is integral to achieving the concept of healing within the garden. A collaborative design among architect, landscape architect, and artist engages aspects of perception and body movement through an awareness and understanding of the human senses. The project reflects the cycles of life, offering a symbolic sense of hope.

A cyclical theme ensures that the experience of the site will differ with each visit depending on the time of day, season of the year, and reason for visiting the garden. In addition to their ability to attract hummingbirds and butterflies to the site, a variety of regional desert plants express seasonal change through color, flower, and scent. Three distinct water features reflecting the cyclical nature of life compose a system of water that flows throughout the site, concluding in the contemplation area. Commissioned art includes tile, glass, and seashell mosaics on nine existing concrete columns and a botanical sculpted steel gate reminiscent of the desert willow tree.

The continuous seat wall offers a variety of opportunities for gathering and interaction. The proximity of plant life falls within the 4"h0" touchable zone.
Photo: Bill Timmerman

Facing page:
A changing watercourse with many voices runs behind the seat wall and represents life's journey. The incorporation of art as a healing element is integral to the design, as seen in the mosaic-clad columns beyond.
Photo: Michael Paulson

A shallow rock pool, "the return," where water flows back into the earth symbolizes life's end. This reflective pool is the centerpiece for the contemplation area, a more secluded place in the garden.
Photo: Bill Timmerman

Photo, facing: Michael Paulson

A changing water course with many "voices" runs behind the seat wall and represents life's journey.
Photos: Bill Timmerman

The contemplation area offers special seating in a more intimate environment. Terraced planters makeenable plant life to be both visible and touchable.

The twelve-story Good Samaritan Regional Medical Center tower building defines the urban context of the site. The hospital tower offers patients a view of the colorful terraced garden below.

Photos: Bill Timmerman

Directory / Project Credits

Casa Victor y Jacinta [p. 14]
Mexico City, Mexico
Architect:
Victor Legorreta
Legorreta Arquitectos
Mexico City, Mexico
525-251-96-98

The Wimberley Home of Healing [p. 20]
Wimberley, Texas
Architect/Landscape Design:
Marley Porter
Living Architecture
Austin, Texas
512-306-0704

Cox-Lindsey Residence [p. 24]
Wake Forest, North Carolina
Architect:
Gail Lindsey, AIA
Design Harmony
Raleigh, North Carolina
919-562-7085

Erle House [p. 28]
Guilford, Connecticut
Architect:
James C. Childress and Paul Shainberg
Centerbrook
Essex, Connecticut
860-767-0175

Builder:
Ron Campbell and Russ Smith
Triangle Builders
Essex, Connecticut

House on Mount Desert Island [p. 32]
Mount Desert Island, Maine
Architect:
Peter Forbes and Associates Architects
Boston, Massachusetts
617-523-5800

Memory Room [p. 38]
Seattle, Washington
Architect/Interior Design:
Olson Sundberg Architects
Seattle, Washington
206-624-5670

Hauptman House [p. 42]
Fairfield, Iowa
Architect:
Anthony Lawlor
Anthony Lawlor Architect
Fairfield, Iowa
515-472-4561

Pawson Residence [p. 46]
London, England
Architect:
John Pawson
John Pawson Architect
London, England
171-419-1200

Exxon Company USA [p. 52]
Brookhollow Campus
Heart of the Campus
Houston, Texas
Landscape Architect:
James Burnett, Lalise Whorton Mason, Rita Hodge
The Office of James Burnett
Houston, Texas
713-529-9919

Interior Architect:
PDR Corporation
Larry Lander, AIA, Drew Patton, AIA
Houston, Texas

Muralist:
Suzanne Sellers
Houston, Texas

Miller SQA Factory [p. 58]
Holland, Michigan
Architect:
William McDonough, Chris Hays
William McDonough + Partners
Charlottesville, Virginia
804-979-1111

Architect of Record:
David VerBerg
VerBurg & Associates
Holland, Michigan

Landscape Architect:
Peter Pollack
Pollack Design Associates
Ann Arbor, Michigan

Interior Design:
Bede Van Dyke, Van Dyck & Associates
Holland, Michigan

The Body Shop Canada Home Office [p. 64]
Don Mills, Ontario, Canada
Architect:
Richard Williams, Steven Quigley
The Colborne Architectural Group
Toronto, Ontario and Vancouver, British Columbia

Landscape Architect:
David Orsini and Associates
Toronto, Ontario

Environmental Designer:
Greg Allen
Allen & Associates
Toronto, Ontario

Electrical Engineer:
Ellard and Wilson Ltd.
Toronto, Canada

Mechanical Engineer:
Keen Engineering Company Ltd.
Toronto, Ontario and Vancouver, British Columbia

Living Machine:
Treatment Process Designer:
John Todd
Ocean Arks International
Cape Cod, Massachusetts

Greenhouse and Treatment Engineering and Construction:
Living Technologies, Inc.
Burlington, Vermont

The Body Shop Canada:
Sean Quinn, Vice-President of Operations
Rifka Khalilieh, Environmental Coordinator

QMR Plastics Facility [p. 70]
River Falls, Wisconsin
Architect:
Julie Snow
Julie Snow Architects, Inc.
Minneapolis, Minnesota
612-359-9430

Outer Circle Products Offices [p. 76]
Chicago, Illinois
Architect:
Jordan Mozer & Associates, Ltd.
Chicago, Illinois
312-397-1133

Design Team Leaders:
Tom Melk, Outer Circle Products
Jordan Mozer and Mike Suomi, Jordan Mozer & Associates, Ltd.

Oklahoma City Memorial [p. 84]
Oklahoma City, Oklahoma
Architect:
Hans and Torrey Butzer
Butzer Design Partnership
Cambridge, Massachusetts
617-491-0655

In collaboration with Sven Berg
Berlin, Germany

Avenue Number 5 [p. 88]
World Expo
Seville, Spain
Urban Planner:
James Wines
SITE Environmental Design
New York, New York
212-254-8300

Gardens, Kobe Nishiokanto Housing [p. 94]
Kobe, Japan
Architect:
Moore Ruble Yudell
Santa Monica , California
310-450-1400

Meditation Space [p. 100]
UNESCO Headquarters
Paris, France
Architect:
Tadao Ando
Tadao Ando Architect and Associates
Osaka, Japan
06-375-1148

Tassajara Bath House, [p. 108]
Zen Mountain Center
Carmel Valley, California
Architect/Landscape Design:
Helen Degenhardt
Helen Degenhardt Architect
Berkeley, California
510-549-6917

Noëlle Spa for Beauty and Wellness [p. 112]
Stamford, Connecticut
Architecture/Interior Design:
Clodagh Design International
New York City, New York
212-780-5300

Kohala Mountain Camps [p. 118]
Kohala, Hawaii
Architect:
James Hadley, Partner
Wank Adams Slavin Associates
New York, New York
212-420-1160

Landscape Design and Preservation:
Patricia Crow, ASLA
Brooklyn, New York

Chopra Center for Well Being [p. 122]
La Jolla, California
Interior Design:
Jean Young, ASID
Young + Co., Inc.
San Diego, California
619-294-9600

Javana Spa [p. 128]
Mount Salak, Java, Indonesia
Owner/Developer/Conceptual Design:
Suhardani Arifin
Jakarta, Indonesia
021-719-8327
626-304-1166 (USA)

Architect:
Atelier 6
Jakarta, Indonesia

Landscape Design:
Darmasto Kusuumanigrat
Kazuhisa Fukawa
Jakarta, Indonesia

Ventana Vista Elementary School [p. 136]
Tucson, Arizona
Design Architect:
Antoine Predock, FAIA
Antoine Predock Architect
Albuquerque, New Mexico
505-843-7390

Architect of Record:
Burns-Wald-Hopkins Architects
Tucson, Arizona

Center for AIDS Services [p. 140]
Oakland, California
Architect:
Elbasani & Logan Architects
Berkeley, California
510-549-2929

Principle in Charge: David Petta, AIA
Project Designer: Guillermo Rossello
Project Architect: D. Jamie Rusin

Interior Design:
Susan Jue
Institute of Business Designers
Berkeley, California

Lighting:
David Makman
Architectural Lighting Design
Berkeley, California

Client:
Rich Levy, Executive Director
The Center for AIDS Services

Contractor:
Stokes Russel Hayden
Berkeley, California

Sinte Gleska University [p. 146]
Antelope, South Dakota
Architect:
RoTo Architects, Inc.
Los Angeles, California
213-226-1112

Principals: Michael Rotondi, Clark Stevens
Collaborators: Brian Reiff, Kenneth Kim, Michael Volk
Project Team: Noah Bilken, Martin Brunner, Marco Brunco,
Carrie DiFiore, Carrie Jordan, Bader Kassim, Jarkko Kettunen,
James Keyhani, Jin Kim, Qu H. Kim, John Maze, Craig Stewart,
James Malloch Taylor, Gudrun Wiedemer, Susanna Woo
Client: Lannan Foundation, J. Patrick Lannan, President
Sinte Gleska University, Lionel Bordeaux, President

Project Management Consultant:
Bruce Biesman-Simons

Structural Engineer:
Joseph Perazzelli, PE
Ove Arup & Partners

Mechanical Engineers:
MB&A, Ove Arup & Partners

Electrical Engineer:
Ove Arup & Partners

Civil Engineer:
Dakota Roadway Consultants, Inc.

Specifications:
ANC/Specifications

Cost Estimating:
Adamson Associates

Other Consultants:
Sinte Gleska University Staff and Community,
Rosebud Sioux Reservation Community

General Contractor:
Scull Construction, Shingobee Builders,Inc.

Timber Framer:
Paul Baines

Therapeutic Garden for Children [p. 154]
Institute for Child and Adolescent Development
Wellesley, Massachusetts
Landscape Architect:
Douglas P. Reed, ASLA
Douglas Reed Landscape Architecture, Inc.
Cambridge, Massachusetts
617-354-0554

Schematic/Conceptual Design and Land Form:
Douglas P. Reed, ASLA, Project Designer
Child Associates, Inc.
Boston, Massachusetts

Hospital Santa Engracia [p. 160]
Monterey, Nuevo Leon, Mexico
Architect:
Henningson, Durham, and Richardson, Inc.
Omaha, Nebraska
402-399-4800

Health and Healing Clinic [p. 164]
Institute for Health and Healing
California Pacific Medical Center
San Francisco, California
Interior Design:
Victoria Stone, MPH, Allied ASID
StoneCircle Design
San Francisco, California
415-826-0904

Art:
Juliet Wood
San Anselmo, California

Sara Glater
Mill Valley, California

Joel Schnaper Memorial Garden [p. 168]
Terence Cardinal Cooke Health Center
New York, New York
Landscape Architect:
David Kamp
Dirtworks, Inc. Landscape Architecture
New York, New York
212-529-2263

Advisory Committee: John Danzer, Bill Dodds, Mimi Ferle,
Jennifer Grey, Peter Karow, Sarah Price, James Ryan, Nancy
Sander, Harry Schnaper, Victoria Sharp, Edwina von Gal

Yacktman Children's Pavilion [p. 172]
Lutheran General Hospital
Park Ridge, Illinois
Architect:
Watkins Carter Hamilton Architects, Inc.
Bellaire, Texas
713-665-5665
In association with Cesar Pelli & Associates
Chicago, Illinois

Beausejor Retirement Home [p. 178]
Aunay-sur-Odon, France
Architect:
N. Malivel, M. Séraqui, S. Arcache
N.M.S. Architecture
Paris, France
1-53-82-8850

Healing Garden [p. 182]
Good Samaritan Regional Medical Center
Phoenix, Arizona
Architect:
Barbara Crisp, Vispi Karanjia
The Orcutt/Winslow Partnership
Phoenix, Arizona
602-257-1764

Client:
Steve Seiler, CEO and Senior Vice President
Good Samaritan Regional Medical Center
Phoenix, Arizona

Landscape Architect:
Kristina Floor and Christy Ten Eyck
Floor & Ten Eyck
Phoenix, Arizona

Clay Artist:
Joan Baron
Baron Studio
Scottsdale, Arizona

Sculptor:
Joe Tyler
Ironwood Botanical Sculpures, Inc.
Sun City, Arizona

Contractor:
Mardian Contractors
Phoenix, Arizona

About the Author

Barbara Crisp is a partner in the architecture firm of
Max Underwood + Barbara Crisp, based in Tempe,
Arizona. She holds Bachelor of English, Bachelor of
Design Science, and Master of Architecture degrees and is
a faculty associate in the School of Architecture at
Arizona State University. The focus of her professional
design work addresses sensory experience and perception
and their relationship to the psychological and
physiological aspects of creating environments that
support and sustain well-being. Barbara lectures and
collaborates in workshops on life-enhancing
environments and healing garden design.